DOLLAR
SIGNS
OF THE TIMES

DOLLAR SIGNS
OF THE TIMES

A COMMONSENSE GUIDE
TO SECURING OUR ECONOMIC FUTURE

R. C. SPROUL JR.

FOREWORD BY R. C. SPROUL

Baker Books

A Division of Baker Book House Co
Grand Rapids, Michigan 49516

Dollar Signs of the Times is a revised edition of *Money Matters* (Tyndale House Publishers, 1985).

Published by Baker Books
a division of Baker Book House
P.O. Box 6287, Grand Rapids, MI 49516-6287

Printed in the United States of America

Library of Congress Cataloging-in-Publication Data

Sproul, R. C. (Robert Craig), Jr., 1965–
    Dollar signs of the times: a commonsense guide to securing our economic future / R. C. Sproul Jr.; foreword by R. C. Sproul.
      p. cm.
    Rev. ed. of: Money matters. c1985.
    Includes bibliographical references.
    ISBN 0-8010-8372-9
    1. Economics—Religious aspects—Christianity. 2. Inflation (Finance)—United States. 3. United States—Economic policy. I. Sproul, R. C. (Robert Craig), Jr., 1965– Money Matters. II. Title.
HB72.S64 1994
330.973—dc20
                                                93-43847

Contents

Foreword

I stared at the television set in stunned disbelief. The hour was late, and I thought perhaps I had dozed off and was experiencing a nightmare. I focused my eyes and strained my ears as the announcement confirmed that stark reality. Bobby Kennedy had just been shot at close range. Pictures of Rosie Grier wrestling with the assailant brought the ugly truth home.

In 1968 I was a theological conservative and a political liberal. I was actively campaigning for Robert Kennedy's bid for the Democratic nomination for the office of President of the United States. His assassination smashed my hopes to ruins. In the 1972 election I wrote in Ted Kennedy's name as a substitute for George McGovern. I wanted Camelot again. I wanted a Kennedy in office, any Kennedy.

My political inclinations in those days were fostered by one chief concern, the concern for social justice. I had studied the Old Testament prophets and was persuaded that concern for the poor and the oppressed must be a passion for any serious Christian. I believed that the only viable instrument to bring about authentic social justice was the federal government. I was sadly aware that with great wealth comes great power and that the super-rich in this country were using their power to influence legislation favoring their vested business interests. I was also convinced that the only way people ever got rich was by exploiting the poor. "One man's profit is another man's loss"—that was the myth that blinded me.

In reality, I was virtually ignorant of the most elementary principle of economics. My awakening came gradually. First

I read William Simon's book, *A Time for Truth*. Simon's analysis of world economic problems and their root causes made me rethink the whole matter of the relationship between theology and economics. Further reading convinced me that some of my assumptions had been in serious error.

Two other major factors entered into my economic conversion. The first was my involvement in the Value of the Person Movement that focused on relationships between labor and management. My time spent in union halls and steel mills gave me a firsthand view of the struggle and pain of America's workers. I began to see that government policies were crippling both labor and management and bringing the nation's steel industry to its knees. Something was wrong, radically wrong. I watched the poor get caught in the vise of soaring interest rates, mushrooming unemployment, and the sudden collapse of once vital industries. My philosophical bent drove me to seek causal answers.

The third factor in my conversion was the influence of my principal tutor in economics, my son. From a young age he was fascinated and absorbed with economic theories. He devoured the complex writings of the Austrian-American genius Ludwig von Mises (1881–1973). He kept asking me questions I could not answer and supplying me with answers to questions I was not even asking. Finally I said to him, "You ought to write a book." So he did.

What follows is what I believe to be a commonsense treatment of economic issues directly affecting each one of us. These issues involve our consciences as well as our wallets, our politics as well as our religious convictions. I hope you will find the book instructive, challenging, and provocative.

R. C. Sproul

Acknowledgments

I have had the good fortune to have been influenced by many insightful people. My parents, who first suggested this project, showed great confidence in me, encouraged me, edited for me, supported my passion for books on the subject, and helped to provide a first-rate education for me. Mr. Henry Hildebrandt, teacher of history and economics at Wichita Collegiate School, sparked my interest with a strong dedication to both freedom and scholarship and provided a solid foundation. His teacher, Dr. Hans Sennholz, served as an inspiration during my years under his teaching at Grove City College.

My peers have also contributed heavily to this work. John Landsverk and Richard White shared this interest with me and sharpened my thoughts through the clash of ideas. Mrs. Julie Smith helped in typing the manuscript for which I am grateful. Thanks are also due to Allan Fisher and Dan Van't Kerkhoff at Baker Book House for believing in the importance of these issues. Finally, thanks to my wife who endured long hours as I worked on the manuscript.

One

Hard Times—
A Christian Approach

"It's the economy, stupid." During the 1992 presidential campaign, Bill Clinton kept a sign on his desk with these four simple yet profound words. Clinton ran against George Bush, the man who had presided over the collapse of the Soviet Union, the most formidable enemy in our nation's history. Bush had swiftly liberated Kuwait from the hands of a tin-horn dictator. The economy was the arena in which Clinton wanted the race run for two reasons. The first was the obvious weakness of his opponent. The second was the supreme importance of the economy in the minds of the voting public.

We are obsessed with the economy. Spend a week analyzing any news medium—television, radio, or newspaper. Note how many stories focus on economic issues. The economy even drives, or influences, non-economic issues. The Soviet Union finds itself on the ash heap of history in large part because it was bankrupted by the arms race. Our leaders' deep concern for the plight of Kuwait was mixed, at least to some degree, with concern for the plight of Kuwait's oil fields. One would think that our national obsession with economics, coupled with the wonders of the information age, would lead us to wisdom, insight, and understanding on economic issues. Instead we are led to despair.

Economics has been called the dismal science, perhaps because it is so confusing. It has been said that if you laid all the world's economists end to end they still wouldn't reach a conclusion. The general public is left confused. What's the difference between the Laffer Curve and a sinking curve? Is the supply side your right side or your left side?

This confusion is no mere abstract concern. Economics is not all esoteric charts and graphs. The confusion reaches into our lives. When the economy stumbles, the unemployment rate grows. The unemployment rate measures real human pain. Unemployment hurts a person's pride as well as his pocketbook. It has become an alarming source of anguish to the American family. Of all economic statistics, this one hits home most brutally.

The 1992 elections focused on the economy. The 1990 tax increase left George Bush vulnerable in two ways. The first was that it spun the economy into a tailspin. The second was that this tax increase coupled with his infamous 1988 pledge of "no new taxes" severely damaged his credibility. (Some have suggested that we read his lips wrong. Perhaps he was appealing to environmentalists who were concerned with the cruel beheadings of tiny lizards, saying "No newt axes.") Bill Clinton promised change. That change turns out to be still more taxes. Another change is Mr. Clinton's commitment to free trade. He used governmental doublespeak regarding the North American Free Trade Agreement, an agreement purportedly designed to open the borders among our neighbors north and south. Instead, free trade was killed by the treaty, dying the death of a thousand qualifications.

Confidence in the future is low. Coming out of the election 57 percent of the voters had no confidence in Bill Clinton. In the first months of Clinton's presidency, that number climbed. The American dream seems as antiquated as a Horatio Alger novel. Our fear, however, seems empty and premature as we observe the economic circumstances abroad. The television beams pictures of starving children with grotesquely distorted stomachs and hollow eyes pleading for help. Eastern Europe struggles to rebuild economies reduced to rubble by decades of communism. Latin America's peasants work without the advantage of adequate tools, adding sweat to their labor beyond the acceptable limits of Adam's curse. Inflation rates creep everywhere, and in many nations gallop, running into hundred and thousand percents annually. Exchange rates fluctuate dramatically. Nations plunge more deeply into debt.

Economic confusion is not merely a Western phenomenon; it reaches all who wish to eat, to produce, to be good stewards of God's creation. Solutions to the confusion are varied and complex, a reality that only adds to the problem. The answers are not easy; neither are they impossible.

Biblical Answers

As popular interest in economic issues grows, Christians have been stimulated to seek biblical answers for economic ills confronting us in the atomic age. Christian bookstores display books expounding the Christian virtues of a socialist state or a theocratic free-market economy. There is a pitched battle in Christendom today fought by radical liberation theologians and militant theonomists (a group hoping for a return to much of Old Testament law), Democrats and Republicans, conservatives and liberals. All claim a concern for human well-being and for firmer biblical roots. Not all, however, are faithful to biblical and economic realities.

As Christians, we bear the responsibility of building a social order that reflects the glory of God. This responsibility reaches into the realm of sociology, political science, and economics. The Great Commission calls for the discipleship of all nations.

We are called to bring the Good News of the risen Christ to everyone and to bring all aspects of our lives under the rule of God. As Americans, we bear the responsibility of making the pledge of "one nation under God" a living reality, a social psalm of praise to God. Only a careful study of scriptural principles and a fervent effort to live by them can fulfill that pledge. This is no time for emotional slogan-writing and name-calling of our Christian brothers in different political/economic camps. We must study together, search out weaknesses and strengths in our own pet system, and strive to bear witness to the kingdom of God.

During any discussion of economics and politics from a biblical perspective, one will inevitably hear the oft-repeated statement, "The Bible is not an economics textbook." No serious economist or theologian would deny this, but its implications are dangerous. The philosophical, moral, and ethical side of economics can easily be overlooked. That the Bible is not an economics textbook does not mean that it is totally useless for understanding economic issues. Economics—in theory and in practice—touches heavily on, and at times rudely collides with, biblical ethics. Where ethics touches economics, the Bible is relevant.

Biblical principles to guide economic study exist. Scripture, though not a textbook, will not leave us groping in the dark, searching for ethical answers with nothing to guide our fallen minds. The Scripture is our guiding force, our given in the study of economics.

Biblical law reaches the totality of life, so we should expect to find biblical principles of conduct for the individual, for the civil magistrate, and for a society. For example, the Old Testament helps us understand the proper function of government and law, important issues in the study of economics. In the New Testament, Jesus dealt with the problem of the poor, the question of wealth, and the role of government. The apostles often dealt with similar questions. In the study of Christian economics, we do not turn first to Smith's *Wealth of Nations* nor to Marx's *Das Kapital,* but rather to the Word of God and the principles therein.

Stewardship

The first principle given to us from Scripture is stewardship. The concept of stewardship is at the root of the word economics. The Greek word *oikonomia,* "economics," literally means "house-law." Economics reaches beyond high-ranking economic advisors, bankers, and professors of economics to all of us who are stewards of this earth. More than the law of marginal utility, more than gross national products and national debts, economics is stewardship, an obligation given to all human beings at creation.

The Bible opens with the creation account. God did not simply rearrange or restructure pre-existent materials left hanging around from eternity. God was no celestial Columbus who discovered the universe and planted a divine flag on it. God brought forth our universe by the Word of his mouth, out of nothing. He owns all things, not through rugged individualistic competition, but from the power of his Word alone. His ownership cannot be contested by civil suits, tax men, or egalitarians seeking equal distribution between Yahweh, Allah, Baal, and Zeus. The universe is neither a corporation nor a partnership. It is a proprietorship, under the same ownership and management from the beginning of time. It is God who creates, and he owns the fruit of his labor.

On the sixth day God created man in his image. Man stood at the apex of the creation, Adam and Eve serving as God's vice-regents. God gave them dominion over the earth; they became his stewards. Their rights and privileges were attended by responsibilities and obligations. Man was given work to do in this first dominion covenant. Adam's work was to dress, till, and keep the earth. This was an economic enterprise. It involved the tasks of production, labor, and stewardship. Note that this responsibility was given in the garden, before the fall. Labor was given as a gift, not as a punishment; it must, therefore, be seen as part of the goodness of creation. Adam and Eve were invited to enjoy the garden, yet at the same time they were called to replenish and keep it. After the fall and expulsion from the garden, Adam and Eve were still given rule over the earth despite their fallen nature. The earth continued to need rule and cultivation, and the mandate of dominion remained.

Man's job is not yet finished. The call to subdue the earth and to be fruitful and multiply still stands despite stunning technological achievements and Malthusian cries of overpopulation. We must take this ancient injunction to heart if we are to be good stewards. We cannot hide our failure in subduing the earth (production) by putting a halt to our multiplying (reproduction). Man abides, and God's mandates abide with him.

God's call to stewardship requires hard work, efficient work, and a high regard for the earth God has given us. God's ownership demands that we care for the earth and use it to fulfill his purposes. We will be held accountable for how well we follow God's commands of stewardship. We must acknowledge and act on our role as vice-regents, as stewards bearing the image of God. We cannot have an ambivalence toward this role if we are to take charge as managers of God's creation in a positive and constructive manner. *Oikonomia* demands that we rule actively in God's house, carrying on the pledge of subduing the earth, being fruitful, and multiplying.

Private Ownership

True ownership of property includes control of that property. In modern fascist states individuals retain legal ownership on paper, while control is dictated by the totalitarian regime. Frederic Bastiat, a French economist of the early nineteenth century, battled against government control of private property in his pamphlets "The Law" and "Economic Sophisms." During Bastiat's time, the French weaving industry was shut down for an entire year as it waited for the bureaucratic word on how many threads per square inch the workers must use. The weavers held deeds to their factories, but they didn't hold control.

This is not merely a phenomenon of the past or of foreign countries either. In the wake of Hurricane Andrew several companies found that insuring homes in Florida was no longer an acceptable risk. The government deemed this not acceptable and ordered these companies to insure the homes and take the risk.

The principle of private ownership of property is woven throughout the Scriptures. Two events took place during the exodus that illustrate the biblical notion of personal property. The first occurred at Mount Sinai with the formulation of the Ten Commandments. The eighth commandment reads, "Thou shalt not steal." Though a relatively simple commandment, it is deemed important enough by God to be elevated to the top ten precepts that establish the foundation of Israel's society.

It is not surprising that a foundational law code for a society would include prohibitions against both killing and stealing. Respect for life and property have been built into countless civil law codes beyond the borders of Old Testament Israel. What is unusual, indeed extraordinary, about Israel's Decalogue is the content of the tenth commandment, "Thou shalt not covet. . . ." How many architects of constitutional law would incorporate into their ten most axiomatic precepts a prohibition of inner lust for another person's property? Calvin sums up this prohibition by writing:

Since the Lord would have the whole world pervaded with love, any feeling of an adverse nature must be banished from our minds. The sum, therefore, will be, that no thought be permitted to insinuate itself into our minds, and inflame them with a noxious concupiscence tending to our neighbor's loss. . . . For if it was correctly said above, that under the words adultery and theft, lust and an intention to injure and deceive are prohibited, it may seem superfluous afterwards to employ a separate commandment to prohibit a covetous desire of our neighbor's goods.[1]

Calvin rightly links the prohibition against coveting with the divine mandate to love our neighbor. Coveting and love are incompatible. Love demands that we refrain from stealing, injuring, despoiling, or even coveting our neighbor's private property. Still we ask, why is covetousness so heinous that it makes the top ten? Consider for a moment the fruits and consequences of human envy and covetousness. Lurking in the coveting heart is the impulse toward theft, violence, vandalism, murder, and war. Eliminate these social ills from our culture, and we will have reduced human suffering enormously.

How can we make sense of vandalism? What does anyone gain by the act of wanton destruction of private or public property? The thief appropriates someone else's property for his own private use or sale, but in vandalism no one gains the property. It is either destroyed or defaced. Yet the vandal chooses to commit his act because it satisfies his hostility toward the property owner. Vandalism is covetousness gone wild. The creed of the vandal is simple, though devastating. He says, "If I cannot possess what you possess, I will destroy it so that you will not enjoy what I lack." The only gain is satisfied hatred.

Ownership of property is sanctioned by God, from the garden paradise to Abraham's flock to the Promised Land to the tents of Saint Paul.

Labor and Property

The Edenic lifestyle was not one of hanging around the garden, acquiring a tan, eating any legal fruit that might fall into one's hands, and chewing the fat with passing serpents. Adam and Eve were called by God to work. And this pre-fall calling gave dignity to labor.

Man was created for work. Luther demonstrated that all callings, within biblical legal bounds, were of value and gave glory to God. Just as the church needs members with different gifts and skills, our world must also have various forms of labor, interdependent and thus valuable. A world full of ministers would be without churches, bread for the Lord's Supper, and printed Bibles to read.

The kingdom of God is a kingdom of craftsmen, and property is the normal result of labor. I find joy as I consider what I have written in this book. The prospect of helping others through this book makes my expenditure of time and energy worthwhile. The fruit of my labor is my reward for carrying out the work mandate.

But many Christian economic systems claiming biblical support do not uphold the connection between work and reward. They view private ownership of property as an evil to combat. Although well intentioned, they can never solve our economic woes. Today's worldwide problems require a strong solution, the very solution proposed by the one who created the world and who knows how it is supposed to operate.

Two

Should Christians Care About the Material World?

For centuries the church has struggled with its understanding of the relationship between the physical and the spiritual, between the body and the soul. Two distortions have plagued us almost from the inception of the church. These twin enemies of biblical truth are radical materialism and radical spiritualism.

Radical Materialism

Materialism is a view of life that regards the possession of material things as the highest good, the summum bonum. It involves more than a mere appreciation of physical things. It goes beyond the simple enjoyment of material benefits. This view is both radical and an ism. It is radical because it makes material things the heart or "root" (radix) of all human happiness. It is an ism because it turns the neutral word "material" into a philosophy of life.

As an ism, materialism declares that the material is all there is. All of life is physical. There is no spiritual dimension. The

consistent materialist allows no room even for the existence
of the spiritual. Thoughts and emotions are explained in terms
of physical and chemical impulses. If nothing apart from matter exists, it follows inexorably that nothing apart from the
material has any value. Indeed even the word "value" must
be given a physical meaning. Values are purely subjective, emotional responses dictated by physical actions and reactions
within the body, a Pavlovian slobbering induced by condi-
tioned responses.

But there are no real materialists in the world, are there?
Surely everyone recognizes that certain vital aspects of life
are in fact spiritual and nonphysical. By no means! From
before the time of Socrates right up to the twentieth century's
B. F. Skinner, some serious philosophers have taken a radically materialistic view of life. (It may be argued that none
have been absolutely consistent. Even Skinner wrote books,
evidently trying to persuade his readers to change their
thoughts through rational persuasion, unless of course he
was counting on the chemical composition of the paper and
ink of the printed page to do the job instead of the cogency
of his argument. Skinner's glaring inconsistency here is like
that of the nihilist who declares that there is no truth and
then writes volumes to defend his own truth and persuade
others as well.)

If radical materialists are few in number, and if even fewer
achieve a consistency of their position, why should we worry
about them? Because the fallout from one philosopher's radical position can affect the lives of millions of people. For example, Karl Marx's philosophical understanding of human history, dialectical materialism, directly affects two billion people
today and indirectly affects the whole world.

However, not everyone thinks about materialism in the complex, philosophical manner of Marx. It is safe to assume that
few people think in complex, philosophical ways at all. Yet
people do think, and thinkers have viewpoints and value sys-

tems. While our value system may not be carefully thought out and we may not be able to articulate it, we do have values, and more importantly, we live by them.

At this level of nonphilosophical living, the world abounds with materialists. The radical sort influences the less radical and more benign sorts. And within this larger camp there are multitudes who believe that life consists of possessions and physical pleasures.

Jesus' parable about the rich fool was not about a philosopher. It was about a farmer who lived as a materialist, with his life caught up in the pursuit of material goods to the point of woeful neglect of his soul. The man was probably not a theoretical materialist. He was a practical materialist, living as if he had no soul.

Practical materialism is seductive. It lures its victims with the hollow promise that the next acquisition, the next pay raise, the next windfall will deliver the prize of happiness. As it seduces, it preoccupies. In reflective moments the practical materialist acknowledges the reality of the spiritual realm and the importance of spiritual values. But he becomes so immersed in making a living that the spiritual is pushed aside by more pressing material concerns.

The stepchild of materialism is hedonism. This ism has appeared under various guises from the sophisticated to the crass. Its creed is simple: Good is equated with the pleasurable and evil with the painful. The goal of the hedonist is to maximize pleasure and minimize pain. The Epicureans who encountered Saint Paul on Mars Hill in Athens were of this persuasion. Theirs was a cultured hedonism, a refined form of pleasure seeking. Still, their creed was without hope: "Let us eat and drink, for tomorrow we die" (1 Cor. 15:32 NIV). The hedonist realizes what the rich fool ignored, the imposing imminence of death. Yet his answer to life is no less foolish.

Radical Spiritualism

The polar opposite of radical materialism is radical imma-
terialism or spiritualism. In this schema the root (radix) of reality is spiritual. From the incorporealists antedating Socrates to
modern-day Christian Scientists, there have always been
denials, or severe depreciation, of physical reality. As with the
materialists, many immaterialists have been more or less sophisticated. Some have adopted this perspective after careful, philosophical analysis while others have accepted it uncritically.

At the practical level, the effect of spiritualism is to depre-
ciate the physical as intrinsically imperfect at best or positively
wicked at worst. Plato's valuing of the soul over the body, the
idea over the imperfect physical copy, has had an enormous
influence on Christian thought. Consider, for example, the
chapter of monastic history where austere forms of rigorous
self-denial, self-flagellation, and other forms of asceticism were
elevated to the status of exalted virtues because of their
antiphysical and therefore "spiritual" bent. The Roman
Catholic dogma of the perpetual virginity of Mary was touched
by this antiphysical perspective. Why else was Rome so zeal-
ous to perpetrate this doctrine apart from the assumption that
even in the marital state the sexual act was somehow tainted
and would blemish the sacred character of the virgin? Even
modern moral theologians argue at times that sex within marriage is at best a necessary evil whose only moral justification
is to reproduce the species. Sex is evil primarily because it is
physical.

But sexual taboos are only a small part of the influence of
spiritualism. It breeds a "taste not, touch not" mentality that
reduces the kingdom of God to matters of eating and drink-
ing, focusing on physical externals as the mark of "true spir-
ituality," a paradoxical measuring rod indeed. Even in today's
Playboy-saturated culture, the cult of the perpetual virgin lives

on. Poverty is glorified, and physical pleasure and beauty are vilified. To love art, music, food, clothes, or private property is to be "worldly." The Roman Bacchanalia is traded in for the hermitage.

A Biblical Alternative

Materialism and spiritualism breed on each other's extremes, fostering endless actions and reactions to each other. The great myth is that we must choose between them. They scream at us, "Either/or, either/or." However, we are not left to choose between these two distortions because Scripture offers a tertium quid, a third option, the notion that matter and spirit are both God's creations, and therefore both good.

The Bible views the material world as the good creation of God. This judgment is more than the simple declaration that God saw it was good (Gen. 1). The Old Testament Jew viewed creation as a voluntary action of God. According to the Bible the world did not evolve or emanate from some eternal substance. God chose to create it by divine fiat. The implication of this for the value of material things is staggering. God chose to create a material world. Within the framework of his own divine mind, he decided to make a world with food and drink and sex. Indeed he circumscribed the use of these physical things by his righteous law. He created them as good, included them in man's fall, and made them an integral part of man's redemption.

The Greek's future hope was redemption from the body. The Christian's future hope is, in part, redemption of the body. The Greek viewed the body as the prison-house of the soul. The Christian views the body as the temple of the Holy Spirit. The Greek viewed material things as being intrinsically imperfect. The Christian views them as good things created by God, though capable of sinful use and abuse.

One of our Lord's teachings has often been distorted to support a false dichotomy between body and soul. We read his solemn words in Matthew 10:28: "Fear not them which kill the body, but are not able to kill the soul: but rather fear him which is able to destroy both soul and body in hell." This teaching seems to imply that men should not worry about the body. What counts is the soul. But Jesus makes no such inference. The contrast he establishes has nothing to do with the value of the body against the soul. Rather it lies between two powers that evoke fear in us: the power of man and the power of God. The one who can kill the body but not the soul is man. The one who has the power to kill both body and soul is God. Man's power to harm us is limited to killing the body. However, the same limit does not apply to God. Jesus' view of the soul differs from the traditional Greek view of the indestructibility of the soul. In Jesus' view the soul is mortal, capable of death. It has what Augustine called the *posse mori*. It cannot be destroyed by man, but it can be destroyed by God. This does not mean that God will destroy the soul as the annihilationists maintain, but merely that he can.

Redemption, in the full biblical sense of the word, is both physical and spiritual. The Bible does not divorce ministering to the physical and spiritual needs of people. The two may be distinguished but never separated. There is, to be sure, a difference between evangelism and a material welfare program, but they should go together.

Recent Christian history has witnessed an unnatural split between these two dimensions of Christian concern. Nineteenth-century liberalism (a distinctive theological movement in the history of Christianity) provoked a crisis by opting for materialism. If, as the liberals supposed, there was no historical resurrection, no virgin birth, no atoning death, no ascension, no miracles, then what was the abiding significance of Christianity in a modern world? What was the church's mission? The liberal church faced difficult options. It could forthrightly apologize to the world for more than eighteen hundred years of propagating error and say, "We're sorry, world, we were wrong. Jesus is dead, and we have misled you with our preaching, our teaching, our music, and our art." This option was preferred by those with a consistent posture of integrity. Some liberal scholars, to their credit, adopted it and left the ministry. It was, however, a radical option and one not very practical for large numbers of clergy. It meant closing the churches, absorbing a monumental financial loss, abandoning a powerful institution of social change, and going out of business.

The liberal church's second option was to focus attention on the relevant, abiding virtue of Christianity—its ethical system. After all, the church was a powerful human institution in a position to influence millions of people in the area of social concern. Of course, this required not only a shift in focus or emphasis of the message of Jesus, but also a massive revision of the content of the New Testament. Scholars sought to penetrate the true essence of Christianity, stripped of its mythical or punitive baggage. What emerged was a social gospel reducing Christianity to a concern for man's present suffering in this space/time world. Now the agenda was to carry out Jesus' mandate of feeding the hungry, giving shelter to the homeless and clothes to the naked, and caring for the prisoner, the widow, the orphan, and all who were poor and oppressed. Christianity was now seen as an ethical force with a social action agenda. The traditional gospel with its emphasis on supernatural, miraculous redemption centering on the person and work of Christ was no longer the key.

This second option left some sticky ethical problems for liberal churchmen. Central to this was the thorny question of honesty in professions of ordination vows and subscription to traditional creeds and confessions. But these problems could be artfully dodged by redefining religious language and gradually changing the content and status of creedal formulations.

The confessions were soon relegated to the status of interesting, but not binding, museum pieces.

Not everyone in the church shared the liberal movement's skepticism toward the supernatural. Conservatives fought fiercely to retain the classical Christology and biblical gospel. Certain fundamentals of faith were considered non-negotiable. The stormy controversy at the beginning of the twentieth century sorely divided mainline Protestant denominations. For the most part the liberals won the day, capturing the strategic seminaries, colleges, and hierarchical positions in the churches and leaving a protracted series of often bitter splinter groups seeking to establish new churches committed to the traditional emphasis of the gospel.

During this stormy controversy, the label *evangelical* underwent a significant historical change in nuance. Originally the term was used as a virtual synonym for Protestant, taking its cue from the Reformation principle of "justification by faith alone." After the modernist/fundamentalist controversy, the term came to signify that group believing in personal, eternal salvation and practicing those forms of evangelism that called people to personal faith in a divine Christ who made a substitutionary, sacrificial atonement and was raised bodily from the grave. (The ideas of deity, atonement, and resurrection were also integral aspects of Roman Catholic theology that, in their essence, were not in dispute during the Reformation.) The evangelical had a new identity and, consequently, a new agenda. He was fighting so hard to retain the gospel of personal salvation as well as his supernatural understanding of Christ that he doubled his emphasis on evangelism, at times to the exclusion of social concern.

And here is where the division occurred. Many thought that the social action agenda of liberalism and biblical literalism of conservatism were essentially incompatible. Evangelicals tended to avoid social reform, now considered a "liberal" concern, for fear of being tarred with a liberal brush. In rejecting liberalism, many evangelicals uncritically rejected social concern, ignoring the biblical mandate for it and the rich evangelical heritage of involvement in it.

The pendulum has swung back. A new social consciousness has arisen among evangelicals that has sparked new interest in social action. The debate now among evangelicals is not so much whether social action is an integral dimension of biblical Christianity but what kind of social action is biblically mandated.

We must also point out in passing through this brief historical reconnaissance that another label used by evangelicals has also undergone a significant linguistic metamorphosis. The term *fundamentalist* has changed dramatically in the last seventy-five years. The term was coined by conservative scholars who entered the debate with liberal scholars concerning the essence of Christianity. The fundamentals were those classic doctrines conservatives believed were the sine qua non of historic Christianity. Over the ensuing decades, however, the term *fundamentalist* took on nuances of anti-intellectualism, legalism, Arminianism, and pietism.

Fundamentalism today as a subculture of evangelicalism exhibits a tendency toward world denial that may obscure the biblical attitude toward physical things. The spirit of Manichaeism lives on, equating the biblical judgment on sinful "flesh" as an implied denigration of all things physical. But even a cursory reading of Scripture affirms that we live in a physical world created by God and that God is profoundly concerned with our bodily lives.

The biblical alternative assigns value to both the spiritual and the material. From Genesis to Revelation the God of Scripture holds out promises of material welfare. Abraham, by divine covenant pledge, was promised that his nation would receive land and property. He became one of the wealthiest men of antiquity, rivaled only by the patriarch Job. The exodus had profound economic overtones. God delivered a people oppressed as a slave-labor force, a people forced into destitute poverty. They were delivered to a land God promised would be flowing with milk and honey, a land where the people could prosper and enjoy the benefits of physical well-being. Here "fleshly" pleasures are promised by God himself.

The imagery of heaven found in the Book of Revelation is replete with signs of physical prosperity and opulence. The new heaven and the new earth, indicating a renovated created order, are crystallized in the description of the new Jerusalem. This city, which comes down from heaven, is adorned with the radiance of rare jewels. It is a city of pure gold with walls of jasper. The foundations are bedecked with precious stones including sapphires, emeralds, topaz, and amethysts. The gates are made of pearls and the streets of gold. The provision of food is a gourmet's delight.

It can certainly be argued that the apocalyptic description above is symbolic and not intended to be taken literally. If these riches were under God's judgment, however, they would hardly be used as symbols of ultimate glory.

The tabernacle and temple structures of the Old Testament were certainly not mere symbols. By divine instruction that included fine details, an exquisite structure was made for the sanctuary. A taste of the details may be found in Exodus 25:1–8.

> And the LORD spake unto Moses, saying, Speak unto the children of Israel, that they bring me an offering: of every man that giveth it willingly with his heart ye shall take my offering. And this is the offering which ye shall take of them; gold, and silver, and brass, and blue, and purple, and scarlet, and fine linen, and goats' hair, and rams' skins dyed red, and badgers' skins, and shittim wood, oil for the light, spices for anointing oil, and for sweet incense, onyx stones, and stones to be set in the ephod, and in the breastplate. And let them make me a sanctuary; that I may dwell among them.

These items for the wilderness tabernacle pale in comparison with the splendors of the temple built in Jerusalem. The temple was an authentic wonder of the ancient world, its glory dwarfing even that of the cathedral of Notre Dame de Paris or Saint Peter's Basilica in Rome.

All these luxurious items were capable of abuse. Indeed, the judgment of God fell on the temple. Israel's silver became dross and its gold tarnished. But there remains a place for these things in God's kingdom. In themselves they are not to be despised. The biblical view assigns value to the body and the soul, to evangelism and social concern, to the spiritual and the material. Redemption is for the whole man.

Three

Prosperity

The Science of Economics

To the uninitiated, economics can sometimes appear incomprehensible. After seeing top experts disagree, many assume they cannot possibly understand it. Although complex at times, economic principles are universally intelligible. And, it is imperative that we have a rudimentary understanding of the science, for it is the study of why there is daily bread on our tables.

Economists study a maze of interconnected forces and try to discover root principles. Adam Smith, history's first economist, devised the "invisible hand theory." Simply put, the invisible hand is the force that takes the combined interests of all members of society and creates a well-ordered marketplace. For Smith, economic forces followed a kind of natural law, a dynamic of checks and balances that functioned without the necessity of government interference or manipulation. Basic laws such as the law of supply and demand worked to keep the marketplace growing. The principles of self-interest balanced by free competition promoted society's interest. Smith understood the reality of sinful human greed but argued that the individual, while acclaiming his own interest in a free and competitive marketplace, frequently promoted the interest of society "more effectually than when he really intends to promote it."[1] (For example, Henry Ford undoubtedly wished to accumulate wealth, while at the same time, many people wanted cheap, accessible transportation. Through this combination, the Model T was born.)

Smith's thought lies behind much conservative economic thought. He is opposed by those who, following the thought of John Maynard Keynes, put the accent on government regulation of the economy. Their theory is that government manipulation, whether by stimulation or restraint, can produce a more ordered and prosperous society than that achieved by the blind forces of nature working in an essentially free market.

Conservatives see the shift from a commerce-oriented marketplace to a politicized marketplace as a disaster for economic growth and prosperity. They argue that what results is a stranglehold on entrepreneurial growth and expansion. If Henry Ford were alive today, they say, he would never get past governmental bureaucratic paperwork. Maybe Detroit would have been zoned residential, or Mr. Ford would have spent his life doing an environmental impact study for the EPA. Perhaps the Model T would have been found "unsafe at any speed." Whatever the case, if Henry Ford had worked under today's restrictions, everyone could have expected a few more years of transportation in the surrey with the fringe on top. According to economic conservatives, the invisible hand leaves a well-ordered market with satisfied producers and satisfied consumers, whereas the highly visible hand of government manipulation leaves welts and bruises on the market and thus on the producer and consumer.

In cutting through the complexities of economics we search for basic, elementary principles that cause economic expansion and contraction. But the intricacies of action and reaction are vast and difficult to sort out. If ever there was a science where the forest could be lost in the trees, it is the science of economics.

Necessary Conditions

In searching for root causes (for these forest-size causes affecting our economic world), we are trying to go back to ground zero to seek what philosophers call the "necessary conditions for something to take place." A necessary condition is that without which something cannot occur. For example, oxygen is a necessary condition for fire, since without oxygen there can be no fire.

There are certain necessary conditions for material prosperity. Only their active use and proper combination can bring forth the desired end—material prosperity. Our quest is for the bedrock factors, the non-negotiables of economic growth.

What conditions must exist for economic growth and material welfare to happen? The first necessary condition is production. Without production we perish. It is a necessary condition, a non-negotiable, a sine qua non of our material welfare. Without production there are no man-made material goods for our benefit. Man can seek to exist by depending on nature's production. He can dwell in caves, forage for wild fruits and berries, and kill wildlife for food and clothing. Yet even these primitive forms of survival methods demand some sort of human production. Primitive tools used for hunting, fishing, cooking, and building are themselves products, crudely fashioned from stone or wood but nevertheless products. Modern material needs such as lumber and bricks for houses, agricultural goods for food, and fabric for clothing provide food, shelter, clothing, and medicine, composing the essential products for survival. They all require production.

It is possible to have production without material welfare if the efforts of production are geared toward useless products. For example, the production of square-wheeled cars adds little if anything to a nation's wealth. For a nation to prosper, production must be of usable goods.

The second necessary condition for material welfare is the development of tools. Tools enable a person to produce more products at faster rates, and they are necessary for increased productivity. Our American steel producers lag behind their Japanese competitors precisely because the Japanese have newer, better tools enabling them to produce superior steel at a lower cost.

Leonard Reed, former president of the Foundation of Economic Education, used a pencil to illustrate the necessity of tools. Reed pointed out that an individual left alone on an island could not produce a single pencil, even if he spent a lifetime trying. However, the hourly production rate of pencils in America is staggering, primarily due to the sophisticated use of tools.[2]

The third necessary condition for material welfare is surplus capital. The purchase of tools requires surplus or investment capital. Without the capital I cannot buy the tools. Without the tools, I cannot increase my production. And without production I cannot achieve material welfare. Yet surplus capital alone is not a sufficient condition for wealth. (A sufficient condition is a condition that is powerful enough, by itself, to cause a given effect.) Surplus capital could be used to invest in tools to produce square-wheeled cars, doing nothing for the desired effect of man's material welfare. Surplus capital must be invested in those tools used for increased production of the goods in demand.

The fourth necessary condition is profit. Profit, though much maligned, is a key to material prosperity because it creates surplus capital. Surplus capital cannot exist without profit. Profit exists when income is greater than expenditure. This simple relationship lies at the root of prosperity: Profit becomes surplus capital, allowing investment in tools for increased production, which in turn produces material prosperity. Of course, profit alone cannot increase prosperity. It can sit idly or be spent wastefully, due to foolishness, greed, or attempts to avoid excessive taxation. Inflation may induce people to consume rather than to save. Profit invested in unwanted goods does not help man's material welfare. Yet prudent investment of profit is the force behind increased wealth.

Consider this illustration.

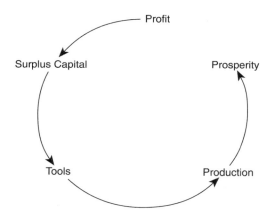

Removing one of these necessary conditions and expecting economic success is like expecting a one-legged man to walk. It simply cannot be done. To enjoy material blessing and to help the poor, Christians must protect these forces from hindrance. We must understand them and study them.

Production

Returning to Leonard Reed's pencil example, let us look further into the relationship between production and material welfare. Imagine that our Robinson Crusoe completes a pencil on his eightieth birthday. If he had worked at $4.35 an hour, labor costs for that one pencil would reach more than $450,000 (assuming sixty years of work at forty hours a week). Today one can buy a pencil for ten cents. Why? Mass production.

In any given production endeavor there are both fixed costs and relative costs. Fixed costs include the cost of land as well as tools. Whether one produces one pencil or one thousand, these costs remain the same. Relative costs are those that change with each additional unit of output. These include raw materials and natural resources. The relative cost of each additional unit is usually low, and this low relative cost means that mass-produced items tend to be inexpensive. As a result, we have an abundance of cheap pencils in America today while Robinson Crusoe has only one.

Mass production in the factory brought on the Industrial Revolution. Though we tend to associate the Industrial Revolution with poor housing and deplorable working conditions for the working classes, we should remember that in spite of these conditions, the proletariat came in droves from the farmlands to work in the factories. Factories engaged in mass production to fill the demands of the workers. And this mass production allowed the common man to have luxuries once owned only by nobles.

The poor reap the benefits of mass production. It strengthens the economy and provides more jobs. Increased production also benefits them by making necessities more accessible. Consider the case of a peasant cotton farmer in an underdeveloped nation. Suppose he is thirty years old, six feet tall, one hundred eighty pounds, and of superior intelligence. Now imagine a Mississippi Delta farmer of the same age but smaller, physically weaker, and less intelligent than the third-world peasant. Why can the Delta farmer produce a hundred times more cotton than the peasant? The answer is not found in brute strength, personal industry, or intelligence quotients. The answer lies with the tools. While the peasant works with his hands, the Delta farmer uses an air-conditioned, stereo-equipped John Deere tractor and cotton gin. His land is fertilized with highly developed nutrients. His cotton is processed in mechanized plants and shipped to the marketplace. The peasant must invest weeks of labor to produce enough cotton for a single shirt; the Delta farmer supplies enough cotton for many shirts every day.

The value to the poor of mass production—production by sophisticated tools supplied by surplus capital—is the lower cost-per-unit of the produced goods. A single shirt is now affordable by most people in developed nations where mass production is used. So it goes with food, shelter, and even medicine. (I once spoke to a medical missionary who ministered to a primitive African tribe whose lives were ravaged by disease, infant mortality, and malnutrition. He stated, "The lives of these people are significantly enhanced by a bottle of aspirin tablets!")

In America today we are in the throes of a productivity crisis. When production falls, our material welfare falls as well. Between the years 1948 and 1954, output (production) per man-hour increased by 4 percent annually. Between 1956 and 1974 the annual increase had fallen to 2.1 percent. In the years 1970 through 1974 the increase stood at only 1.6 percent annually. By 1980, for the first time in American history, our productivity actually decreased. According to William Simon, writing in *A Time for Truth,* from 1960 to 1980 the United States ranked last in productivity growth among eight major industrialized nations.[3] The once robust United States economy has grown weak on a diet of excessive taxation, monetary inflation, massive federal debts, and governmental regulations. No economy can survive long, let alone grow, in such an environment.

Productivity is more than an abstract word used by demanding executives and scientists. It goes beyond pragmatic growth programs and material welfare. Productivity is a spiritual and ethical obligation. We are called to be productive by God. God commands that we "bear fruit," that our work be worthwhile. Paul's exhortation that those who do not work shall not eat (2 Thess. 3:10) illustrates our obligation to produce. We must bear fruit so our hungry will be fed and our nation may be blessed with prosperity.

For production to take place, three things are necessary: time, energy, and money. I reached an understanding of this as a teenager at the family dinner table. Our grass had been quite productive during springtime and as a result needed to be cut. My father explained that he had neither the time nor the energy to perform the task. He was, however, prepared to reward me handsomely with his money in exchange for my youthful abundance of energy and time. It was the start of a prosperous business relationship.

My father supplied the lawnmower. The lack of a mower would have altered the relationship dramatically. The time and energy used in cutting the grass would have increased one hundredfold if I had had to cut the grass with a pair of scissors or, worse yet, with my front teeth. To make it worth my while, my wages would have had to increase significantly. The lawnmower is a relatively simple and inexpensive tool, yet it enables work to be done more easily, more quickly, and at a lower cost. One simple tool gave my family a beautiful yard, me a relatively painless job, and my father an inexpensive laborer. It saved me time and energy while saving my father money. That small amount of money saved could improve the all-around economy in various ways. It could be spent elsewhere to help someone else's business or it could be invested, privately or through a bank, to finance more tools elsewhere in the economy.

Control of tools is the key to production. In any given production endeavor, tools carry the most weight. The common equation, land + labor x tools = wealth, emphasizes the importance of tools to production.

As an energetic young boy I often participated in neighborhood baseball games. Because they were unorganized with no official umpire, there were many disputed calls. If the debate over a call could not be resolved, the final decision was turned over to the tool owner, the child who had provided the bat and the ball. This boy was the highest authority because he had the power to halt play completely by going home, bat and ball in hand. Here I learned the axiom, "He who controls the tools controls the game."

Karl Marx had much to say about the ownership of the means of production. The Communist movement was rooted in two basic assumptions concerning tools. Marx's theory of surplus value stated that profit is the theft of the worker's fruit of his labor. He argued that the value in a given product lies in what the worker puts into it. But the laborer receives wages equal to the value he produces in only a fraction of his working day. The remaining value, produced in the rest of his working day, is skimmed off the top, stolen by the propertied class. To redress this exploitation of the worker, Marx called for national ownership of the means of production. He regarded private ownership as an evil causing the misery of the working class. Marx failed to see the true source of economic value.

Value is determined, not by man-hours, but by the desires of the consumer. The square-wheeled car illustrates this principle. The process of producing such a car would no doubt necessitate long and strenuous labor. However, consumers would pay little for it despite the enormous "value" instilled in it by the producers' blood, sweat, and tears.

Tools

Profit results when the consumer places a value on a given item higher than the cost of producing the item. The producer bets that his product will be in great demand. He invests his money in the tools of production, hoping he can satisfy the needs or whims of the buying public. Tools keep the cost low and the profit high. Marx failed to see this actual role of tools in the production process. Tools save both the bourgeoisie and the proletariat time, energy, and money. Tools are the force behind production. These savings allow mass production at low cost and in turn allow the common man to experience treasures never imagined before the Industrial Revolution.

The ownership and control of tools constitute control of the production process. Private control tends toward efficiency, while bureaucratic, governmental control brings inefficiency and a distortion of the market process. The Communist experiment in Russia showed us misery and starvation, not a worker's paradise. A study of history shows the vast difference in material welfare between economies based on private industry and those based on government control. Automation leads to high, more efficient production. While it may temporarily dislocate jobs, in the end it leads to high employment. Tools work, and they must be protected from interference if we are to enhance our material welfare.

My grandfather often delighted in explaining to me the way things were before I was born. Before the advent of power steering, truck drivers generally had arms large enough to make Charles Atlas envious. Turning the wheels of such large trucks was no easy task. Today, Charles Atlas's mythical ninety-seven-pound weakling could turn the wheel of the largest trucks with relative ease. Truck driving is open to more men and also to women because of a tool—the powered steering wheel. The most monstrous man in a pre-power-steering truck was far less efficient than a ninety-seven-pound weakling in a more modern truck. Physical strength is no match for superior tools.

Archimedes, the ancient Greek mathematician and physicist, understood this point long before Adam Smith walked the earth. Archimedes did not say, "Give me arms strong enough, and I shall move the world," but rather, "Give me a lever big enough, and I shall move the world." Tools can have the strength of a thousand men. They never get tired. Some may bemoan the loss of seeing the truck driver flex his big arms as he makes a turn. I cheer the new freedom of power steering and leave the big arms for Charles Atlas.

But the desire to work hard cannot alone bring us higher productivity. Just as physical strength is no match for good tools, an industrious spirit by itself cannot beat good tools for higher production. Even if we give great industrious zeal to our strong man driving the ancient truck, the weak man in the modern truck would remain more efficient and productive. Although zeal and physical strength are desirable, tools are the most potent and necessary ingredient in productivity.

Government ownership of the means of production has not alleviated the misery of the common worker. If anything, it tends to increase it. Government cannot be efficient and work properly in the marketplace, because it is an agent of force. And because it cannot use the pricing mechanism as a gauge of supply and demand, it need not make a profit, it need not be efficient, it need not be productive. The American education system illustrates the point.

We live in an era of rapid technological growth. Modern science is meeting the demands for newer and better tools. The computer, the word processor, and better forms of communication are increasing efficiency in the office. In the factory, robotics is growing, causing some to cheer and many to worry that this new form of automation will raise unemployment. Such fear is not new. Throughout history many have decried machines for taking away jobs. Yet the record indicates the opposite: increased productivity increases employment. To be sure, specific jobs are lost, and some people are forced to relocate their employment, but these are only a temporary cost of increased production.

A good illustration of the relationship between productivity and employment lies with the shipping industry, once the

leading industry of the northeastern United States. This industry centered on whaling, since oil processed from whales was
the leading commercial substance used in lamps to illumine
American homes. Almost overnight the industry went belly-
up. What happened? Mr. Drake dug a hole in Titusville, Penn-
sylvania, and discovered oil. The first commercial use of the
new "black gold" was kerosene, a cheap and efficient fuel for
oil lamps. While oil men experienced a boom and produced a
generation of Jed Clampetts, things were bad in New England,
as harpooners were suddenly out of work, their skill no longer
an economic necessity. But the kerosene boom itself was short-
lived. The oil industry was suddenly threatened by a man
named Tom Edison who in effect said, "A pox on all your oil
lamps." Unemployment hit the kerosene plants, while business was soon booming at Sylvania and General Electric. For-
tunately the oil tycoons received a stay of economic execution.
The combustion engine and Henry Ford used new forms of
production that insured the oilmen a lucrative future. (One
wonders what would have happened had the government
poured money into salvaging the whaling industry or restraining the building of cars or light bulbs!)

Automation does not take jobs from the market, but rather
allows the mass production that in turn raises employment.
Let me illustrate. Sir Richard Arkwright invented his cotton
spinning machine in 1760. At that time in England there were
approximately 5,200 spinners and 2,700 weavers using spinning wheels. In all, 7,900 labored in the production of cotton
textiles. But Arkwright's invention met bitter opposition
because workers feared losing their jobs. This opposition was
so violent it had to be put down by force. In 1787, Parliament
studied the number of workers spinning and weaving cotton.
The study revealed that 320,000 persons were earning their
living spinning and weaving in 1787 as compared to 7,900
just seventeen years earlier. This represented an increase of
4,400 percent.

Yet today many economists still support the idea that automation hurts employment rates. Some economists are concerned about the booming computer industry. They claim it will cause a loss of jobs in our country and decrease the demand for labor. These economists apparently conclude that we can maximize jobs by making labor inefficient and unproductive.

An economics teacher of mine once shared with the class his plan for full employment. The way to end unemployment is simple, he told us; we need only eliminate the wheel. Every unemployed or underemployed man, woman, and child could then be hired to carry wheat on his or her back from the heartland around the country. No more trucks, cars, trains, bikes, or airplanes. Without the wheel we would enjoy full employment.

Tools do not grow on trees. Modern tools are often intricate, delicate, and expensive. One cannot walk into the local hardware store and ask for a bottle-capping machine. Tools must be made to order, to do their assigned jobs in a particular place in a production line in a given factory. Tools must be tailored to their individual purpose. Industrial tools, for the most part, cannot be mass-produced, therefore their costs run quite high. At the same time, the demand for tools is enormous. To stay in business, an owner must keep abreast of the latest technology in order to continue to grow in efficiency. As a result of this great demand and their high value, large industrial tools tend to be very expensive. Here we see the initial role of surplus capital.

Surplus Capital

Surplus capital is money put aside for the purpose of investment in tools. It is essential for a company to compete and to grow. Any attack on surplus capital is ultimately an attack on productivity and, therefore, on the material prosperity of the nation as a whole. Erosion of surplus capital creates damage no social program can fix.

The Japanese today incur the wrath of many Americans. Everything from bumper stickers to television commercials implores us to "buy American." The simple fact is that they are outcompeting us. They produce better cars, better steel, better motorcycles, and better radios. Are they to be blamed? Japanese quality is often attributed to their industrious spirit, their lower wages, and their lifetime hiring practices. The most crucial factor, however, is that the Japanese have superior tools. (One example is their auto industry with far more robotic equipment and other tools than our own.)

These superior tools are made possible through one thing—investment capital. From the sixties through the early seventies, private investment in the United States averaged less than 18 percent of the gross national product per year. During that same period, Japan averaged almost twice that amount with 35 percent per year. From the sixties to the early seventies, the United States was lowest in capital investment among all industrialized nations. These are not irrelevant statistics. This kind of investment and a desire to serve the consumer make a company profitable. This is bread and butter. From 1960 to the early eighties the United States ranked last in productivity growth among the eight major industrialized nations also. The correlation is obvious. We, as a nation, are not fulfilling the biblical mandate to bear fruit. It is not a case of a nation resting on its economic laurels, but rather of a nation suffering from governmental policies that discourage the accumulation of surplus capital. Without the surplus capital there can be no tools. Without newer and better tools, our productivity—our fruit-bearing—is dealt a fatal blow.

Taxation hurts the accumulation of surplus capital. Many producers pay little or no tax at all through the use of tax shelters. It appears that investment is not taking place because so much money is being poured into frivolous tax shelters and that wasteful consumption is the culprit responsible for our declining productivity. The effect of taxation and money put into shelters is essentially the same: Money taxed or sheltered cannot be used for productive purposes.

Economist Arthur Laffer, supporter of supply side economics, introduced a solution to the problem. The Laffer Curve illustrates the effects of taxation.

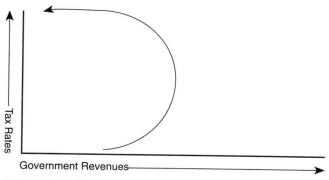

THE LAFFER CURVE

Laffer suggested that two different tax rates produce the same amount of income. A zero percent tax rate brings no income. A 100 percent tax rate brings no income either, since all taxable activity ceases due to a lack of motivation. In like manner, a 10 percent tax rate brings in a similar amount of money as a 90 percent rate. The lower tax rate could bring in sufficient income to run the government and still give the people the incentive to save and be productive. Conspicuous consumption, the spending of great wealth on frivolities and baubles, would cease, and more money would be poured into the production process.

Wasteful consumption does not come through stupidity or greed, but rather from governmental practices of taxation and inflation that make it unprofitable to save money—money needed for tools, tools needed for the productivity that brings material prosperity. The Laffer Curve cuts the Gordian knot of government growth and private stagnation. In the years following the Reagan tax cuts, federal revenues actually increased.

Profit

Profit is essential to material prosperity. It is at the base of those factors that are non-negotiables for material prosperity. It is a necessary condition for material welfare, allowing savings for investment in tools and production leading to wealth. Without profit, there is no money for investment. Profit makes growth possible.

Profit is also more than one company's balance. It is a family's balance. When a family spends less than it earns, the profit can be turned back into the family. The breadwinner or winners can invest the money in education, making their skills more marketable. Their profit can be used to purchase a more efficient automobile, making travel more efficient. A family's profit can be used for investment in businesses. But taxation and inflation make saving difficult for the family.

In all its various forms profit is the basis of all human action. In every endeavor, from reading Scripture to buying a new television, one expects to experience a net gain, whether monetary, spiritual, or intellectual. You picked up this book expecting to gain, or profit, from it.

Profit is the basis for all commerce. In any voluntary exchange, all participants profit. Historically, profit has been thought to be a zero-sum interaction; that is, anything gained by one is lost by another. But a careful examination of commerce shows this to be a fallacy.

Suppose one boy is not willing to trade his Willie Mays baseball card for less than one dollar. We can say he values that card at one dollar. Also suppose this boy loves bubble gum and would part with $1.50 for a hundred pieces. Another boy might pay $1.50 for a Willie Mays baseball card, but would care little for the hundred pieces of bubble gum. He would give up his gum for a dollar. These boys meet and trade their goods. Before the transaction, there was two dollars' worth of value in the two boys' possessions. After the trade, there was three dollars' worth of value—each, in a sense, profited fifty cents in value from the trade.

Conclusion

Economics is an important and relevant field of study. As Christians we must look for the forces that will encourage and protect our prosperity. We have seen the relationship of four of these factors: production, tools, surplus capital, and profit. We have looked at some historical and present-day obstacles, such as the widespread but erroneous belief that tools cause unemployment, Marx's misguided theory on profit, and the taxation of profits. Understanding economic forces helps us build a social order in agreement with God's plan as well as his command to be good stewards of the earth and to bear much fruit.

Four

Profit Is Not
a Four-Letter Word

The word "profit" today has a bad ring to it. It has become a six-letter obscenity. Just as "rugged individualism" has turned "individualism" into an ugly word, so also have adjectives such as "indecent," "exploitive," and "obscene" given the word "profit" a bad taste. While actual profits average less than five cents on the dollar today, public opinion polls show that Americans believe companies make thirty-five cents in profit from every dollar of sales revenue. Consumers bemoan the losses of major industries whose quarterly reports are summarized on newscasts and at the same time are filled with rage at reports of the profits of large oil companies. We sympathize with those unproductive, inefficient producers who don't have the skills to meet public demand while cursing those who do meet the demand and are rewarded for it. We view profit as a little chunk of each consumer taken coldheartedly by the producer.

But profit performs an important role in the marketplace. Without hope of some kind of profit, there is no reason to work. Profit is a monetary pat on the back for a job well done. It acts first as an incentive. Profit is why we get up to go to work in the morning. With no hope of profit, Henry Ford would not have started the automobile industry. Necessity is not the mother of invention; profit is.

As we saw in chapter 3, profit allows the accumulation of surplus capital needed for investment. It acts as a gauge for future investment. When a producer makes large profits, investors step in to compete. Today, ninety years after the first Model T rolled off the line, Americans can choose from over twenty-five car manufacturers. Had Ford not made a profit, not only would there be no competitors, but Ford himself would have moved on to producing something else! Lack of profits likewise alerts investors to stay out of a field that lacks significant demand. Profit is not a necessary evil—it is an important cog in any free-market wheel.

The Nature of Exchange

To understand profit we must understand the nature of exchange. Ultimately only two things can be exchanged, goods and services. Money is not valuable in itself, but it has trade-in value for goods and services. Money is a promise for future goods or services. Exchanging goods or services directly, without using money, is called barter. Money makes the exchange indirect, as the money is later exchanged for goods and services.

If I sell my car for money, I may spend that money later on a motorcycle. In effect I have bartered a car for a motorcycle. In this exchange, I value the money (or its purchasing power) more than the car. That is profit. The buyer of my car values the car more than the money. That is profit. All voluntary exchanges therefore end in mutual profit. Any coercive trans-action is not true trade, but theft. Should the government wish to build a highway through my yard against my wishes, what-ever my reimbursement, that is an act of theft. Freedom is the key to profit, as only voluntary exchange insures mutual profit.

There is widespread confusion in our culture about the nature of profit. Trade and profit rest on the subjective nature of value. No person can impose a value on something that he himself does not value. At a recent economics seminar a professor asked his audience the question: "If a shoemaker spends forty dollars to make a pair of shoes and then goes to the marketplace and sells his shoes to a customer for fifty dollars, who makes the profit?" The vast majority of the audience gave the same answer—the shoemaker. In a business exchange, entered into voluntarily, however, this answer is only partially correct. The full answer is the shoemaker and the customer.

There is no objective value to a pair of shoes. In a bartering society, the exchange would take place something like this. The shoemaker produces fifty pairs of shoes. He has no need for fifty pairs of shoes, but he does need food. He therefore has a surplus of shoes and a scarcity of food. The shoemaker prefers to eat steak, even if it tastes like shoe leather, rather than trying to make shoe leather taste like steak. Meanwhile back at the ranch, the cattle rancher has far more beef than he can possibly eat, but his toes are cold. He, therefore, has a surplus of food, but a scarcity of shoes. The rancher then takes his beef to the shoemaker and makes a deal, exchanging his beef for shoes. In this transaction, both trade one commodity for something they value more highly at the moment and in their particular circumstance. In this exchange both profit. They each get what they value more in exchange for what they value less. If this were not so, the exchange simply would not take place.

However, something happens to our perception of an exchange when the transaction takes place with the use of money. Money is an indirect means of exchange, more sophisticated and complex than the direct method of barter. Because of this indirectness, the mutual, reciprocal benefit of barter is obscured. The illusion is created that one party (the seller) profits, while the other party (the buyer) loses. In barter, it can be said that both parties are buyers and both parties are sellers. It is no different with an indirect exchange. Behind the apparent legerdemain is the fact that the shoemaker sells his shoes to the customer in exchange for money and the customer "sells" his money to the shoemaker in exchange for shoes. Both sell. Both buy. Both profit.

This illusion of one-sided profit is enhanced by the public searchlight beamed on business profits. Businesses must report their profits and losses to the IRS, to their shareholders, to corporate boards, and so on. The individual must report all of his income to the government. He is not required to report all of his purchases. Yet, in reality, for both businesses and individuals, purchases are as much profit as wages.

A recent conference in Chicago featuring economists from the University of Chicago focused on economic problems of development in third-world countries. At one point, an agitated member of the audience complained that the rich people were buying up all the land in India. The sentence hung in the air as a self-evident accusation of gross injustice going on in India, of the rich exploiting the poor.

The speaker asked, "Is the land for sale in the marketplace?" The answer was yes. "Then, what is unjust about a rich man buying land that is offered for sale in a free transaction?" The acerbic cloud hovering over the original question was suddenly blown away.

But doesn't profit result from greed and the exploitive opportunism of one party taking advantage of another person's need? Isn't there something inherently dehumanizing about the marketplace? It is true that no Christian can afford to neglect the devastating power of greed. There are cases of exploitive opportunism such as selling a canteen of water to a person dying of thirst in the desert for a million dollars. But what Adam Smith so astutely understood was that the free market is the best check and balance system for curbing the distortions of greed and exploitation. Greed cannot be profitable unless the greedy man's products are sold. In a free market the customer determines the price of the goods, not the greedy seller. If the customer doesn't want the greedy man's goods he simply won't buy them. If the greedy man succeeds, he will do so only if his greed indirectly benefits his customers by serving their needs and wants. If a seller seeks to profit exploitatively by charging "too much" for his goods, the second Smithian plank of balance comes into play—competition. Even in the desert an exploiter can get his million dollars for a canteen of water only until someone else shows up to offer it for half the price. In a free market, competition forces the greedy to reduce prices or go out of business.

Still we are left with the question of one person's taking advantage of or profiting from another person's need. The maxim of free bartering or free market exchange is "From each according to his surplus, to each according to his wants." This could also be translated into "From each according to his surplus, to each according to his surplus." What lies behind this is the principle of division of labor, and this principle assumes the social character of humanity. It assumes that no human being is ever totally self-sufficient. As God has ordained things, there is a diversity as well as a unity to the human race. Just as in the church the eye cannot say to the ear, "I have no need of thee," in the marketplace the farmer cannot say to the shoemaker, "I have no need of thee." A marketplace of voluntary exchange actually promotes humanity.

However, coercive collectivism, where the state's power forces a kind of uniformitarianism, discourages individuality and the entrepreneurial spirit. Not only does history record the massive economic failures of collectivism, it also indicates that where economic freedom is lost, political freedom perishes with it. In such a system the inherent diversity of human gifts, vocations, and personalities is quenched. Hordes of Chinese people work at the same jobs and dress the same way as a symbol of their enforced uniformitarian condition. In a free market I can wear plaid or tweed, blue jeans or three-piece suits. I can be a butcher, a baker, or candlestick maker at my own discretion.

In voluntary exchange, profit can never be obscene or exploitive. I may pay more than I want to pay for a given good or service, but I never pay more than I am willing. Should I pay $100 for a painting costing ten dollars to make, I am not being gouged or exploited. I am making a profit, for I value the painting more than $100. Before we curse the business with which we make our exchange, let us remember the nature of trade and mutual profit. We are the ones who place value on the goods we purchase and on the goods we don't purchase. No one can make us buy anything we do not want (with the possible exception of the government). In a free market we buy what we want and thank those who produce what we want.

Prices are not determined by a producer's vice-president for consumer affairs or by the custodian. Prices are determined by us, the buying public. The producers must sell a maximum number of units of a given good at a maximum price to attain maximum profit. Let us imagine that it costs Mr. Hershey twenty cents to make a candy bar. If he sold these bars for twenty dollars, he would probably profit nothing as few people would pay that much. If his candy bars sold for twenty-one cents, he could sell perhaps a hundred thousand bars a day, profiting a thousand dollars a day. If these bars sold for twenty-five cents, and eighty thousand bars were sold per day, Hershey's profit would amount to four thousand dollars a day. When we see a twenty-five-cent candy bar on a counter, we must cast our economic vote. A yes vote means we exchange the quarter for the bar. A no vote, and the quarter remains firmly ensconced in pocket or purse. The price that yields the highest profit is the price at which the producer will sell the product. The amount of profit rests solely on the amount people are willing to pay for any given object.

The marketplace is not a place of totalitarian dictators; it is a democracy where a dollar is a vote. In the end, the majority rules. If our favorite automobile has been taken off the market, perhaps it is because the dollar votes weren't there—not enough people bought the car. The consumer is the supreme ruler of the marketplace, able to bring out new products and get rid of old ones with the simple spending of his dollar.

Producers do not produce junk and tell us to take it or leave it. They are suitors, vying for the attention of the spending public, aiming to please, to fill demands. Producers are not just trying to get by. The producer understands he must please the consumer more than his closest competitor does. When it hurts to buy something, we must remember it's due to our indecision in the voting process, not the fault of the producer. If prices get to us, we should blame the consumers who pay them, not the producers who are simply responding to their value system.

What should we do if the prices for commodities are higher than we want to pay? Should we turn to government to bring the prices down? Governments have frequently interfered with the market price. And this has almost never produced a net gain for a given country. Price-fixing has never brought anything but hardship because it moves the consumer out of his rightful position as ruler of the marketplace and puts Big Brother in his place. Price-fixing doesn't fix anything; it only creates problems.

The Market Price

Economists speak of the "market" price for a given good. This is the price set without government interference. Let us assume that the market price for all candy bars is twenty-five cents. The government fears that at this price the poor will have to live without the candy bar (something so un-American that

it would be unpatriotic to deny it to anyone). The president
signs into law a bill requiring that all candy bars be sold for
fifteen cents or less. This is called a price ceiling. We can expect
one thing to happen immediately—candy bars will sell out!
Rich, poor, Republicans, Democrats, everyone will enjoy that
great American delicacy, the candy bar. But the following day,
there will be no candy bars. None. Why would anyone produce candy bars at a loss? The government's plan to allow
everyone to enjoy the candy bar results in no one enjoying the
candy bar.

The net result of any price ceiling is always shortage. Government price ceilings on gasoline caused lines to grow to
enormous lengths while production went down. Why drill a
new oil well when one can't make any profit on it? Price controls take the incentive out of investment and cause great shortages. No profit, no investment, no tools, no production, no
wealth. Price ceilings designed to help the poor only hurt them
and everyone else as well. History has proven this again and
again. The market price allows for the best distribution, as
those who want things the most pay for them. Those who do
not care are not hurt.

Government price-fixing also comes in the form of price
floors. These are designed to keep people producing "necessary" goods. The farming industry is heavily influenced by various price-floor schemes today. Price floors are government-
induced (forced) prices set artificially above the real market
price. Let us assume that the market price for a bushel of wheat
in any given season is two dollars. The government, in order
to protect the farmer (and win his voting support), will make
any price below three dollars a bushel illegal. This a price floor.
As a result, thousands of young people, seeing farming as an
area of great profit, head for the great outdoors to start their
farms. Production skyrockets, and sales plunge. The result is
an enormous surplus. Tons of grain slowly rot in elevators
throughout our country. Soon the government steps in to cor-

rect the problem it created by promising to buy all unsold wheat. As a result, the farmer celebrates while the budget and tax rates grow, along with the wheat.

Government schemes to affect prices have always been with us. The bad side effects of such policies remain also. However, the real price, the consumer price, can always be found somewhere. When the price of a commodity is artificially controlled, freedom truly reigns in the black market. There, one can find a candy bar despite the shortage. The black market is the free market because it is beyond the power of taxation, price controls, and regulation. Government can pick at and harass the marketplace, but it cannot destroy it as long as people can produce and place value on goods and services. Governments rise and governments fall. The free market always survives.

Fraud and Coercion

Governments have been exploiting people since the time of Amos, the poor man's prophet. Amos chastised Israel for its exploitive practices and promised the coming judgment of God. Amos 2:6 reads, "Thus saith the LORD; For three transgressions of Israel, and for four, I will not turn away the punishment thereof; because they sold the righteous for silver, and the poor for a pair of shoes." Selling the righteous for silver refers to the practice of unscrupulous judges receiving bribes, the act of declaring the innocent guilty for monetary reward. Selling the poor for a pair of shoes was Israel's second indictment. The Jewish nation had no bankruptcy laws; all debts were paid in full. If one man could not pay what he owed, he would temporarily become his creditor's slave. This was not practiced to cause humiliation, but rather to be certain that all debts were paid. The judges at the gate of the city would assess the debtor's value as a laborer. These judges often attributed absurdly low values, the price of a pair of shoes, to the labor of the debtor, thus enabling the creditor to squeeze out as much labor from the debtor as possible. The debtor was robbed of his labor by the low value attributed to him. These practices hurt the poor man most, who could not find justice in the gates of the cities of Israel, God's chosen nation, and they brought God's judgment down on Israel.

One must remember that Old Testament Israel, the only nation with its constitution and law written by God, had no bureaucratic agencies to regulate and interfere in the market. The government's involvement in the market was limited to stopping fraud and coercion.

The most common kind of fraud mentioned in the Old Testament is the use of false weights and measures. When selling, a merchant could cheat by using a weight that would measure out less than the customer paid. When buying, he could obtain more than he paid by using a false weight. Deuteronomy 25:13–16 reads:

> Thou shalt not have in thy bag divers weights, a great and a small. Thou shalt not have in thine house divers measures, a great and a small. But thou shalt have a perfect and just weight, a perfect and just measure shalt thou have: that thy days may be lengthened in the land which the LORD thy God giveth thee. For all that do such things, and all that do unrighteously, are an abomination unto the LORD thy God.

Leviticus 19:35–37 likewise forbids the use of false weights and measures.

There are only two ways of acquiring what could realistically be called obscene profit: fraud and coercion. Fraud is not the result of a high percentage of profit but of dishonesty. Coercion is a more obvious form of illicit profit. Coercion comes in the form of theft, extortion, robbery, and often taxation. The thug trades protection (from himself) for money. He profits through the threat of violence or death. We do not enter the social security scheme voluntarily but through coercion. We are offered, in a most humanitarian way, freedom from want in our old age. In the meantime, we are taxed, our children are taxed, our neighbors are taxed, and our parents are taxed, while legions of bureaucrats and politicians profit illicitly.

Force and fraud are two evils with no place in the free market. They are subtle forms of slavery that rob the victim of the fruit of his labor. The Scriptures deplore these evils and implore government authorities to fulfill their proper role in stopping them. Whether in the form of a finger on the meat scale or a gun at our back, they are violations of the God-given right to private property.

Only two groups are capable of effecting coercive exchanges of goods and services: criminals and governments. The essential difference between the two is a matter of legality. It is illegal for the robber to steal my property at gunpoint, but it is legal for the government to do it. This is seen most clearly in the principle of eminent domain.

The *Dictionary of the Bible* defines the right of eminent domain as "the power of a government over all the property within its limits, by which it is entitled to appropriate, or to authorize the appropriation of, private property for public use, giving just compensation to the owner."[1] The problem with the principle of eminent domain lies in the last clause of its definition, "giving just compensation to the owner." Here, the theory goes, property is not stolen as in common theft. It is purchased at a "just" price. Nevertheless, it remains a coercive exchange, "justified" by being for the common good.

The problem is this: It is never, never, never possible to transact a just, coercive exchange. Why? In a coercive exchange the owner is forced to sell his property at a lower value than he puts on it. Remember the subjective basis of value. There may be a going market price for land, but that does not affect the value a person places on his own property. This market price provides him with a barometer of the value others may put on his property if he chooses to sell it, but in a free market his decision to sell or not to sell remains his. If the government offers to buy his land and he desires to sell it at the offered price, then the compensation is just. But if he is forced to sell when he does not want to sell, he has been coerced into parting with his property at a price less than the value the property has for him. Thus, a coercive sale can never be just. If the government offers the property owner ten times the market value but the man values his land at eleven times the market value, he has been robbed. Eminent domain is a government's legal license to steal. When the property owner resists the attempt of the armed robber to steal his goods, he is a hero. But if he resists the government's coercive seizure of his land, which comes at a gunpoint far more sophisticated and potent than that used by the common burglar, he is a criminal.

The infamous Old Testament King Ahab indulged in the use of eminent domain:

> Naboth the Jezreelite had a vineyard, which was in Jezreel, hard by the palace of Ahab king of Samaria. And Ahab spake unto Naboth, saying, Give me thy vineyard, that I may have it for a garden of herbs, because it is near unto my house: and I will give thee for it a better vineyard than it; or, if it seem good to thee, I will give thee the worth of it in money. And Naboth said to Ahab, The LORD forbid it me, that I should give the inheritance of my fathers unto thee.
>
> 1 Kings 21:1–3

When Ahab reported Naboth's refusal to his wife, Jezebel, she replied with obvious sarcasm, "Do you now govern Israel?" Jezebel conspired to bring false charges against Naboth in the courts, and Naboth was summarily executed. We read: "And it came to pass, when Ahab heard that Naboth was dead, that Ahab rose up to go down to the vineyard of Naboth the Jezreelite, to take possession of it" (1 Kings 21:16).

Ahab acquired the vineyard, but in the deed he received also the curse of God. Elijah pronounced God's judgment: "Thus saith the Lord, Hast thou killed, and also taken possession? . . . In the place where dogs licked the blood of Naboth shall dogs lick thy blood, even thine" (1 Kings 21:19).

The parallels of Ahab's action with the principle of eminent domain are evident, but there are some significant differences as well. The appropriation of Naboth's land was for private gain to the king, not for the public good. Second, Naboth was executed on false charges rather than punished for violating the law. The king did seek private, personal gain, but his act was not strictly a private matter. In a monarchy the king is a persona publica. In his office he embodies the public. In a sense the gain of the king is construed as a public gain. Here the clear distinction between private good and public good is obscured.

That Naboth was executed on false charges is also significant. It indicates that Israel did not have a law of eminent domain to serve Ahab's interest. He tried to purchase Naboth's vineyard. When Naboth was unwilling to sell, Ahab had no authority to confiscate his property. The story tells of the abuse of government power and the provocation of the unmitigated wrath of God.

Covenant

Since God first promised Adam and Eve paradise in Eden in exchange for obedience, he has been making and keeping covenants. From Adam to Noah and his rainbow covenant to Abraham and the covenant of salvation, God has faithfully kept his promises despite the disobedience of his people. Our God is not a fraudulent God. He is a covenant maker and keeper.

The covenant principle is a simple one: One party promises something in exchange for the promise of the second party.

Various penalties are to be paid in the event of the violation of the covenant. The prophets from Elijah to Malachi warned the Jewish people of the coming sanctions for the violation of the covenant.

The covenant principle operates today, not only in a religious sense, but in the marketplace as well. The modern-day contract is a covenant. Contracts are like covenant promises to fulfill a given task in exchange for another task. A contract is our assurance that there will be no fraud, that we will get what we pay for.

Yet our culture reflects a society where covenants are easily broken. A wildcat strike, for example, is a violation of the covenant, or contract. The marriage contract is maintained only about 50 percent of the time; almost one in two marriages ends in divorce. But contract breaking is a violation of the ninth commandment, a form of fraud. Christ's words echo the ninth commandment, "Let your communication be, Yea, yea; Nay, nay: for whatsoever is more than these cometh of evil" (Matt. 5:37).

The Value of Labor

Critics of a free market assume that profit necessarily results from oppression or exploitation of the worker. Karl Marx complained that profit alienates the worker from his labor, arguing that it is the owner who profits, not the worker. The owner gets rich at the expense of the laborer.

This issue of the value of labor was brought up during the strike of the National Football League's Players Union that forced an abbreviated season in 1982. One of the heated questions in the strike centered on distribution of revenues earned from television. The players wanted a piece of the action, participation in ownership. Their argument was simple: They were the performers, the gate attraction that brought in the revenue.

Without them there could be no profit. In addition, they were the ones risking injury to their limbs while the owners enjoyed the comfort and safety of being spectators.

The disagreement touched on a complex array of economic and moral questions. The owners argued from an economic platform, saying that (1) the players were salaried employees working under contracts they had agreed on; (2) labor has no intrinsic right to profits above and beyond the salaries; (3) labor's market value is determined not by effort, but by supply and demand; and (4) the players did not participate in the capital risk of the endeavor and should therefore not demand a portion of the capital gains of the enterprise.

In the marketplace, labor is a commodity, bought and sold just like goods and services. We might wish that people attached more value to our labor than they do. Indeed we may argue that they should do so. But these considerations have little effect on the marketplace, where the law of supply and demand reigns supreme. If there is a glut of schoolteachers, the value of each teacher decreases. If there is a scarcity of schoolteachers, their value increases, provided, of course, that there are people who want education.

The same is true of football players. The NFL players' argument that they were the ones people paid to see had to be balanced by the fact that there were thousands of aspiring football players who would have loved to take their places. There was competition for their jobs. To be sure, they had secured their roster positions by convincing the owners that they were the best available performers and that their replacements would lower the quality of the team performance the public paid to watch. This is what gave the players their bargaining power. On the other hand, the owners must know at what point it becomes unprofitable for them to give the public the best possible product. They may be induced to provide lesser thrills for lesser labor costs if their profit margin declines.

At a men's prayer breakfast at Willow Creek Community Church near Chicago, all-pro defensive back for the Chicago Bears, Doug Plank, related the following anecdote: When reporting to training camp, he was amazed to discover he was being paid for what he loved to do for fun. He wasn't in the league long before he learned that his employers wanted something in exchange for his pay. At the end of the season the Bears were winning a game against the San Francisco 49ers when their star running back made a long run to beat them in the closing seconds. He broke six tackles on the way to the end zone, including one by Plank who was playing safety. As he started off the field, Plank could see the fury gleaming in his coach's eyes. "Plank! We're paying you $65,000 to make that tackle!" the coach screamed. Doug looked the coach in the eye and retorted, "I know, Coach, but San Francisco is paying him $800,000 to break that tackle!"

Salaries in a free market are determined by a business transaction that is a form of trade. The services of the individual are sold to the company at a price agreed upon by both parties. If it is a free transaction, no one is exploited. Marx failed to understand this when he complained that a wage earner is a kind of slave. To be sure, there is usually more money to be made in ownership than in wages, but there is also more to be lost. The salaried employee trades a degree of freedom for a degree of job security.

The difference between a slave and a free wage earner is this: In a free market the worker is free to do the kind of work he chooses, to seek employment with the kind of company he prefers, to live where he chooses, and to quit his job if he chooses. He is even free to become an entrepreneur. In slavery the worker's work is selected for him; where he lives is determined for him; he is not allowed to quit. In a word, he is owned.

The risk factor of ownership is often overlooked, especially when successful owners receive so much attention in the public eye. Consider the story of Art Rooney, who invested his private capital in the Pittsburgh Steelers. For forty years Rooney's team never won a division championship. The ledger book of his company was literally sprinkled with red ink. The fans stayed away from football games while screaming their frustrated slogan, S.O.S. ("Same Old Steelers"). Then came the seventies and four Super Bowl championships. Suddenly Rooney owned a bonanza. Season tickets sold out years in advance. The present crop of players who risked none of their capital over that forty-year span wanted a piece of the ownership. Rooney was not disposed to give it to them. He vividly recalled the absence of players clamoring to participate in his losses during the lean years.

Conclusion

Profit, at any rate, barring force and fraud, is not an evil. It is the result of the level of demand by consumers and voluntary exchange. Government attempts to tamper with profits disturb the balance between supply and demand, creating surpluses, shortages, and injustices, profiting no one save the government. Profit is not only not evil, it is good, driving the market and serving producers and consumers alike.

Five

What Money Can Do

Barter

The earliest free trade probably took place soon after the first instances of fraud and covenant breaking. Satan's great sale had taken place, and Eden was an old memory to Adam and Eve. The earth was beginning to be populated. Men were leaving their crude homes in search of the day's food, equipped only with an empty stomach and a few stones.

One man stayed behind to work on his new idea. He had seen a once ferocious lion virtually paralyzed by pain from a small thorn in his paw. The man lashed a small stick to a sharp stone and designed the world's first spear, a jumbo thorn. The following morning, our ingenious young man left his cave early and returned shortly, dragging a large deer with the monstrous thorn in its side. The other hunters gazed in wide-eyed wonder at their hermit-like friend who was beaming proudly beside his kill. The following day the inventor constructed two of these newfangled spears, and gave them to two neighbors in exchange for a portion of their kill. Barter was born.

Barter is the exchange of goods or services for other goods or services. The first trade took place in barter form. The process of barter did much to alleviate economic misery. It also heralded the advent of division of labor. The newfound abundance of meat made possible by the technological breakthrough of the spear allowed others to leave hunting for businesses of their own. Some people produced weapons while others hunted. They worked on animal skins or pottery; they chopped firewood. There were no spear control laws, no taxation of profits, no barter fixing to interfere with the wealth of these early men.

Barter flourished as its benefits became apparent. Our imaginary hermit could invest his time finding sharper stones for constructing spears. The growth of the hunting industry gave the hunters greater purchasing power. As a result, other industries grew as well. After the hunt everyone gathered to trade wares. Hunters had to locate the finest meats, makers of clothing had to identify the softest and warmest skins, and woodcutters had to find the best-burning trees. Once everyone had huddled, hungry and cold, in damp dark caves; now they were enjoying the luxury of a filling meal, warm clothes, and a fire. All this resulted from the idea of one lonely man. Barter allowed the accumulation of these luxuries, encouraging people to work harder and smarter. People began to search for better tools and develop more efficient work habits.

Although barter was a great breakthrough in the production of wealth, its power and scope were limited. One had to find someone who not only wanted what the first had, but also had what the first person wanted. The spearmaker grew tired of trading for meat. The hunter grew tired of trading for spears. Sometimes barter could be arranged through three parties: The skinmaker wanted meat, the hunter wanted a spear, and the spearmaker wanted a skin. The hunter could trade his meat for a skin, then trade his skin for a spear. Everyone was happy, but the transaction took a great deal of time and energy.

Besides, barter neared its limit in the three-way deal, since it was almost impossible to come up with four or more producers with compatible interests and the time or desire to arrange such a complicated deal.

Our hermit, the great economic thinker of his community, searched long and hard for a solution. After many sleepless nights it dawned on him—clay tablets! He entered the market the following day carrying a bundle of high quality spears and an armful of clay tablets. The tablets bore this inscription: "The holder of this tablet may redeem it for one spear." A frustrated skinmaker approached the hermit, bemoaning the limits of the barter system. The hermit, whose skins were threadbare, offered a tablet to the skinmaker. "But I have no need for a spear right now," the skinmaker explained. The hermit suggested that someone undoubtedly would need one in the near future, someone who perhaps had something the skinmaker would want. The two made a deal. The skinmaker traded a skin for the tablet (which he redeemed for a small bear before the day was done). Eventually all producers installed tablets into their market proceedings. Thus the beginning of money. Trade boomed beyond anyone's wildest imagination. A shoemaker, a butcher, and a water gatherer started new businesses. The men prospered. Tablets were used more and more as the community soared to new heights in prosperity. Trade was no longer restricted to two or three people. Now, tablets could reach each producer before being exchanged for their real worth.

Once again growth leveled off and the community paused on a new plateau. The problem? Each person valued his products differently. If the skinmaker only wanted a pound of meat, he didn't want to trade a full skin or the right to a spear. The community turned its eyes to our hermit friend who had grown old and wealthy since his original spear venture. Again he racked his brain for a solution. Suddenly he saw the answer! Rather than clay tablets, he would find something divisible. The next day at the market he put up a sign at his booth:

"Spears for Sale, One Tablet or Fifteen Beads." Soon all trading was done in beads: seven beads for a pound of deer, twenty-five beads for a new skin. Trade boomed once more, and the community thanked our genius hermit, who retired to write down his discoveries for other communities around the region.

The value of money lies in its acceptance as an indirect medium of exchange. The power of money is that it can be traded; it can be exchanged for goods and services. Money is the go-between, the middle man in the exchange of goods and services. To have any value, money must be acceptable in exchange for goods and services. If the skinmaker had wanted meat, but the hunter had been unwilling to accept the beads, the skinmaker would have been a pauper. His beads would have been useless.

As long as the money supply remains stable, the power of money remains relatively stable, no matter how many times it exchanges hands. (The effects of an unstable money supply will be examined in the following chapter.) Money is like the power of a river driving any number of mill wheels: The power is not affected by the number of the people through whose hands it flows.

Whether beads or gold, money acts as a catalyst to trade in the marketplace by allowing more transactions to take place. As we examine the idea of mutual profit in all voluntary exchanges, we see that money adds to a nation's wealth, not in itself, but by facilitating more transactions and thereby increasing profit.

What Money Is Not

To understand what money is, we must first examine what money is not. In itself, money is not wealth. It cannot feed, shelter, or clothe man. It cannot offer physical comfort to anyone. Imagine yourself on a desert island. After your ship sinks, you manage to reach a tropical island with clothes on your back and a suitcase full of neatly piled hundred-dollar bills. You cannot eat the money; you cannot shelter yourself with it; and you cannot clothe yourself with it. You cannot buy protection from lions and tigers and bears. You cannot buy a return ticket home with it. You are left with a suitcase full of daydreams of what might have been. Robinson Crusoe, on a nearby island, might be penniless, but he enjoys the wealth of food, clothing, and shelter that would take you years to accumulate as you produce the bare necessities of life. Wealth lies in the ability to produce, not in beads, shells, rocks, paper, or gold.

Money is also not a fixed measure of quantity or quality. The five-thousand-dollar automobile of 1910 was inferior to the two-thousand-dollar automobile of 1952. The ten-thousand-dollar house of 1910 was superior to the ten-thousand-dollar house of 1947. In 1932 a dollar bought five times as much wheat as it did in 1952. The same dollar that represented a hundred pieces of gum to you as a child represents fifty pieces of gum today. Money, even under the gold standard, is not altogether stable in its purchasing power from one time to another.

If a bottle containing fifty pieces of bubble gum were to wash up on the beaches of Robinson Crusoe's island, your money would be as useless to Mr. Crusoe as it would be to you. You cannot suddenly declare that your dollar is worth fifty pieces of gum. Tomorrow it might be worth five hundred pieces, or ten. Tomorrow the gum could be of such quality that you would exchange your dollar for only one piece, or perhaps you would want no gum at all.

Thirdly, money is not always pieces of paper or metal. Today most of the money in circulation is bank credit, seen only in the form of bank checks. Such forms of money flow easily through computers, making the cumbersome process of cash transfer less common and less necessary.

And finally, money is not a claim against goods or services, nor are goods and services a claim against money. The exchange depends upon the willingness of those owners of particular goods and services to trade with the owners of money. Money claims nothing. However, it can be traded for goods and services under any situation of mutual consent.

The Evolution of Money

Money changed its form with the passing of time. Beads were one of the earliest forms of money. Other products such as shells, rocks, sticks, skins, and feathers were used as well. As man cultivated the soil and tamed animals, commodities such as grain, oil, dried fish, tortoise and cowry shells, sheep, horses, and especially cattle were used as mediums of exchange. The ox, one of the most marketable of all available goods, was a popular medium of exchange in the ancient world, used by ancient Greeks, Hebrews, Romans, Arabs, and others up to the late Middle Ages.

As the division of labor spread and urban development began, cattle money was slowly phased out in favor of the metals then in use. With the advent of metal handicrafts, copper, bronze, gold, and silver became the most widely accepted form of money. Precious metals were first used as money in the form of weapons and ornaments. As these metals became more widely recognized, they began to be used as raw materials rather than as finished goods. As trade over the known world grew, so did the acceptance of these precious metals. Gold, silver, bronze, and copper became the money of civilized people. These precious metals were extremely useful in the marketplace, making trade less cumbersome. They could be easily divided and transported at a low cost, allowing the expansion of trade over large areas of land. They could also be stored with relative safety unlike the earlier perishable mediums of exchange, such as grain and meat.

However, one serious inconvenience remained with the use of metals in the marketplace. Each transaction required constant testing and weighing of the metals. To solve this problem the Lydians of Asia Minor in 650 B.C. began to use coins. The Greeks soon followed. Coins became small pieces of metal with a visible mark of guarantee for their weight and fineness. Paul Einzig, author of *Primitive Money,* proposes that coinage may have been invented during the late Mycenaean period from 1400 to 1100 B.C.[1] This coinage system is believed to have perished with the Mycenaean civilization. Precious metals have been made into coins continuously from 650 B.C. The early coins were made of a natural mixture of gold and silver. Later coins used bronze, copper, pure gold, and silver. The early coins carried a variety of symbols and portraits. The Roman coin of the early first century bore the face of Caesar. It followed the Roman armies and was used in trade throughout the empire at the time of Christ. We recall the attempt of the scribes and chief priests to trap Jesus when they asked him,

> Is it lawful for us to give tribute unto Caesar, or no? But he perceived their craftiness, and said unto them . . . Shew me a penny. Whose image and superscription hath it? They answered and said, Caesar's. And he said unto them, Render therefore unto Caesar the things which be Caesar's, and unto God the things which be God's.
>
> Luke 20:22–25

Coins became the most popular medium of exchange all over the world and constituted universal money until the beginning of the twentieth century. As barriers separating coinage systems were broken down, trade prospered. As trade prospered, so did the material welfare of those involved in the trade. Profit possibilities were magnified enormously.

And as trade grew, coins changed dramatically. Any metal used in trade must maintain a delicate balance of scarcity and plenty. If a metal is too common, its value is eroded and it fades out of the trading process. If a metal is too scarce, it soon loses acceptability and also fades out of the trading process. Before too long, the common metal copper dropped out as a major medium of exchange. Bronze soon followed. Silver and gold became the universal means of exchange.

Money from precious metals was the market medium of exchange up to the first half of the twentieth century and coins were manufactured both by private and public mints. The oldest coins were probably issued privately to meet the requirements of markets or firms. Soon governments, seeing this as an area of possible profit, joined in the manufacturing of these coins. The governments were successful in this endeavor, but their success was limited by the competition of private mints. To remove this barricade, governments began to outlaw the private manufacture of coins used in trade, and they created for themselves monetary monopolies.

In the contemporary situation, governments around the world are the sole coiners of money. The proposition that private companies could coin money is so foreign to modern man that it is often thought to be an economic impossibility. Yet few governments in history have been able to resist the temptation to use their legal power over money to their own advantage. From early history rulers have been known to clip their coins. Later governments put holes in the centers of their coins, claiming it necessary for identification. These actions served to devaluate the coins and cast a shadow over their integrity.

Mercantilism

As the glory of gold spread, nations began to value gold more than the goods they could purchase. This led to the fallacy of mercantilism. Mercantilism arose as an economic movement in Europe in the eighteenth century based on the premise that a country should attempt to sell more than it buys in order to accumulate gold. The fact that useful goods and services constitute real wealth was obscured. Nations began to sell goods and services all over the world, but to buy only at home, storing up gold and silver. The fallacy of this system is quite apparent. Gold is not of great use apart from trading. Nations can use only so much gold for weaponry and ornaments. Nations that accumulate gold can enjoy its shiny splendor while nations that trade, buying goods with gold, can enjoy the products they purchase.

Wealth is goods and services. And money is not wealth. Gold's primary value is that it can be traded for any goods around the world. Sitting gold, gold not being used as a medium of exchange, is basically useless. Sitting gold is like a stream that has been redirected around the mill wheels to build a pool of water. The pool is nice to see, but it won't help you produce.

American industries have resorted to the myth of mercantilism by running to the government and asking for protection from Japanese competitors who sell their goods within our borders. Former president Reagan, for example, raised the import duty of foreign motorcycles to protect America's sole producer, Harley-Davidson. Americans are fearful because our country is not selling enough outside its borders and buying enough inside. Americans today are caught up in the counterproductive game of mercantilism, and we are losing.

Trade, by definition, is equal and can contain no deficits. Yet news commentators periodically report to us the latest figures on trade deficits. Trade deficits are a contradiction in terms in a free market. Mutual profit is the result of every trade transaction. Imagine a sportscaster reading the score of a baseball game between Japanese and American all-stars, "America lost its game with the Japanese today by a score of 5 to 5." The idea of trade deficits violates the law of noncontradiction. When John Q. Public of Middletown, USA, buys a car from Toyota of Japan, this "unpatriotic" man has just caused a worker in Detroit to lose his job. That is trade deficit. What can Toyota do with its new American dollars? Only two things—put them in its vault and look at them or spend them. If the money remains in their vault, America has one more car and Japan has more paper. The only other option is to spend the money. American dollars, any nation's dollars, will all ultimately be spent in the nation that produced them. The money comes back to America. There is no deficit because trade, whether through barter or indirectly through money, is always equal. Import tariffs do not save American jobs, they merely save the jobs of inefficient producers at the expense of efficient producers who produce that which other countries want. Though long since refuted in Adam Smith's *Wealth of Nations,* mercantilism is flourishing as an economic system even though people cannot prosper because of it.

It is a continuing battle. Throughout the 1992 presidential campaign, and into his presidency, Bill Clinton waffled on the proposed North American Free Trade Agreement. NAFTA claims to open the borders for free trade among our North American neighbors. It is, however, riddled with protections for many industries. To the degree that borders were truly opened, NAFTA created enemies, including producers who sell primarily in the U.S. and those who labor for those same producers. These are the people who are protected by protectionist measures. Those who are most hurt are those who produce goods sold overseas. For every auto worker whose job is saved by tariffs on foreign cars, there is a farmer who loses his job because he cannot sell to a particular country. The pain, however, spreads throughout the economy. Only a madman would suggest that the U.S. economy is better served by its citizens paying more money for inferior goods. Free trade allows individuals and nations to produce that which they are best able to produce.

Mercantilism, though a strong and destructive force, did not stop trade and the use of gold as the medium of exchange altogether. However, gold did eventually give way to paper as the medium of exchange. Paper, like the tablets, could be exchanged for gold but it seems an odd form of exchange for gold. Gold, having scarcity and being in demand, has market value while paper is plentiful and renewable. Nevertheless, paper has come to be used as the medium of exchange in the market.

Why did people accept paper rather than hard money? The reasons for a change from gold to paper are relatively simple. Imagine yourself as a baker working hundreds of years ago. Stashed in your house is one hundred units of gold but this gold can be stolen. Wanting to keep the gold safe, you deposit it in a warehouse. The warehouse owner gives you a receipt. Your neighbor, the butcher, places a hundred units of his own gold in the same warehouse and receives a receipt. The butcher then wishes to buy a loaf of bread from you at a cost of one unit of gold. He could walk to the warehouse, ask for a unit of gold, return to you, and pay his one unit of gold. This, of course, is an extremely inefficient way of doing business. Another method would be through the exchange of receipts. A receipt for one piece of gold for one loaf of bread could take place within the bakery without the wasteful walking back and forth. This was how paper money began in the marketplace.

Paper money—certificates of deposit—circulates endlessly through the economy. However, behind the paper is always this promise: The paper can be exchanged for its corresponding gold value. The acceptance of paper as a medium of exchange lies in the fact that it can be, at any time, exchanged for a scarce commodity, gold.

If Rip Van Winkle had gone to sleep in 1962 with a fistful of dollars, he would have held in his hands a promise of an exchange for silver. In 1962 the U.S. dollar could be redeemed at any time for silver. If Rip woke up today and headed to his bank with his old and wrinkled dollars, he would receive only a puzzled look when he asked for silver in exchange. Today our money bears the promise of nothing. Paper money is no longer a certificate of deposit of anything because it has no hard value behind it. Rip would now have to accept the payment of his debt in paper dollars.

What is behind paper money now is government force. Paper money in America today bears the words "legal tender," meaning that debtors have the legal right to pay all debts in paper money. This system works within the borders where the government has the power to enforce its legal tender. Outside those borders the value of the paper fluctuates according to people's confidence in the promises of the government that issues the currency.

The specter of Gresham's Law contributes to the economic instability of many of the world's nations. The law, simply stated, declares that "bad money drives out good money." Good money tends to be hoarded rather than circulated. Try an experiment. Reach in your pocket for a quarter. Drop that quarter on a counter. How does it sound? Now pick it up and read the date on it. Is the coin dated before 1964? Surely it isn't. If it were, you would want to save it rather than spend it. Why? Because the silver content of the coin could be sold at more than its currency value. That is the simple reason that pre-1964 coins are no longer in circulation. If you own such a coin, continue the experiment by dropping it on a counter. Listen to its ring and compare it to the dull thud of the coins of recent vintage. Gresham's Law works.

Bad money that is produced from cheap materials causes an economy to go "thud." Bad money not only drives out good money, it drives prosperity away. The entire American economy is supported by bad money, paper-thin paper dollars. Eventually confidence in such bad money will collapse, and bring the economy tumbling down with it.

Six

The Inflationary Rip-Off

Imagine Gallup pollsters taking to the streets armed with paper and pads and posing this question, "What is inflation?" Chances are a sizable majority will answer, "Higher prices." This answer reflects a serious misconception fostered in part by a government campaign to take the heat off themselves and place it squarely on the back of the business community.

One man explained the riddle of inflation to me in this manner. A butcher grows tired of owning only one automobile. To raise the money for a second car he raises his prices. The plumber, in order to afford the butcher's high prices, likewise raises his prices. The mechanic, in order to pay his plumbing bill, raises his prices. This process continues throughout the community.

But if this chain reaction occurred in a marketplace with a stable money supply, no one could buy anything. If the money supply remained the same while prices escalated, the money supply would not fit the number of available goods and services. In a stable supply situation, the butcher who first raised his prices would lose his business to other butchers who were satisfied with one car. It is the consumer, not the producer, who sets the price in a free market. If the butcher wants a second car he must do his job more efficiently and provide for

81

the consumer better than his nearest competitor. By raising prices merely to satisfy his own desires, he would quickly price himself out of business.

My grandfather often talked about the prices when he was a young boy. Fifty years ago, movies were a quarter, candy bars a nickel, and the best New York strip steaks were little more than a dollar at his favorite restaurant in downtown New York City. Prices have changed dramatically, but the rise is not inflation, it is the result of inflation.

Inflation is not the change from a five-cent candy bar to a fifty-cent candy bar. It is the increase in the money supply. The quantity of money is inflated, resulting in a proportionate deflation of the unit value of the currency. Government figures on inflation, the consumer price index, are not a measure of inflation, but rather a measure of the effects of inflation. Inflation comes from the government printing office, not from business. The government covers its tracks by pointing to the producers, rather than by announcing its monthly increase in the money supply. Government is the only possible source of inflation (except for counterfeiters).

Not too long ago, the American dollar could be exchanged for a given amount of gold. The American dollar was a receipt for gold, just as clay tablets were once redeemable in spears. Our dollar was backed by history, by a standard of the past, by 150 years of hard, stable money. However, today's American dollar is redeemable in dollars and nothing else. Our government gives us only currency, a currency with no hard value, paper with nothing to stand behind it.

Economists, "gold bugs," calling for a return to hard money, are anachronisms, lonely prophets heard by few and heeded by still fewer. Even the defenders of free enterprise, the renowned Chicago school led by Nobel Prize winner Milton Friedman, have renounced the gold standard and are calling for limited inflation and a controlled level of fiat currency to stimulate a stagnated economy.

Imagine a tiny mythical country with ten loaves of bread and nothing more. This country has ten units of currency with each loaf of bread being equal in value to one unit of currency. A printing press is introduced into the country, and this press cranks out ten more units of currency. Now each loaf of bread is worth two units of currency, as there are ten loaves and twenty units. The price has doubled. But the wealth of the country remains the same. There are twenty units but still only ten loaves. The salaries of the citizens would no doubt double. No one would be any richer because production would remain the same.

The doubling of the currency proves to be a useless, but harmless, folly. However, the effects of inflation on a nation can be far more serious. The process that begins with production, produces surplus capital, and leads to material prosperity is damaged with the introduction of inflationary practices. If the money supply is doubled, the value of the money held before the doubling is cut in half.

Let us suppose you are the proprietor of a very successful business. As you satisfy the demands of the buying public, profits pour in. In order to make your business more successful, you hope to invest in the latest machinery to produce your product. You diligently save your profits. But their value plummets as the government printing press increases the money supply. The value of your savings falls. It is folly to save in such an environment because the longer you save, the lower your money value drops. If you earn 5 percent interest on your savings and the annual inflation rate is 10 percent, you have a net annual loss of 5 percent. You quickly pull your money out of the bank and spend it. Inflation pressures the consumer to spend, spend, spend. But such saving is folly, both for the business proprietor and for the family. Families cease to save, and a serious depletion of surplus capital occurs. As we have seen, if surplus or investment capital diminishes, investment in tools declines, production falls off, and the wealth of the nation falls.

This reaction is integral to the Keynesian system designed to stimulate consumer spending. Consumer spending, you will remember, is essential to material prosperity. An increase in consumer spending due to inflation sends false messages to producers, leading many to believe they need to expand. But this increase is due to the declining value of paper money and not to increased wealth or production. Such an increased demand is an illusion. As in the mythical ten-loaf town, the extra ten dollars didn't signify more production, just more paper. Had the bread factory assumed higher demand and stepped up production, a lot of bread would have gone stale.

Banks learn quickly also. If a bank lends money at a rate of 8 percent, and the inflation rate is at 10 percent, the bank is losing money. It is receiving its payment in devalued money. Inflation does not mean easy money for borrowing. Instead, inflation necessitates high interest rates to cover the loss of receiving devalued money. At the same time, increased consumer spending causes a shortage of loanable funds resulting in still higher interest rates. With skyrocketing interest rates and inflationary incentives to spend and not save, investment in the tools of production drops. The end result is a decrease in material prosperity.

A Counterfeit

Inflation eats away at the core of material prosperity, capital investment. It is like encouraging someone to eat and then taking away the means of producing food. The rich are not buying jewels, yachts, furs, and works of art because they are greedy as much as because these goods devalue more slowly than their paper money in the bank. Do not blame the rich, blame the government that cannot practice the first law of house-rule—don't spend more than comes in. Blame the government that believes consumption rather than production is the key to prosperity. Blame the government that eats away at the savings of its citizens. And blame the government that sets itself above its own laws and the laws of God by practicing policies that debase its people's currency.

The news reports tell about budget deficits, federal reserve plans, appropriations, stopgap spending, and the consumer price index. But one word is glaringly missing—counterfeiting. And this is precisely the problem—legal counterfeiting.

Suppose that each year I write out a projected budget for the coming months. My annual income is $12,000. My annual expenditures amount to $14,000. I project a $2,000 deficit. In a dark, musty corner of my basement lies the solution to my problem: a printing press. Every night I quietly print crisp, one-dollar bills to cover my deficit. These bills bear the words "legal tender," and they are accepted everywhere I go. My budget now balances. My conscience is soothed by remembering that $2,000 in fake bills increases consumer spending and helps our ailing economy. The next year, due to inflationary pressures, my income is upped to $15,000, but my expenditures reach the $20,000 mark. I am forced to work longer hours in my damp corner to cover this $5,000 deficit. But I rejoice in stimulating the economy.

One day two policemen come to my door toting guns, handcuffs, and a search warrant. I enter the police station handcuffed but smiling. However, I do not fear imprisonment.

I arrive at my trial and as my own counsel, I stand to speak. "Your honor, ladies and gentlemen of the jury, I stand before you an accused man. I am charged with counterfeiting. I stand guilty. Guilty of following in the noble tradition of the red, white, and blue, guilty of patriotism, guilty of helping our ailing economy. Send me to prison if you will, but you must also send our leaders of state, the counterfeiters for the cause of prosperity. Send also the citizens who elected our leaders to do this great deed of counterfeiting. Send the American nation to prison, for if I am guilty, we are all guilty. The defense rests."

The judge then offers me ten years of rest in a federal prison, and I am relieved to awaken from my nightmare in a cold sweat.

The problem with government counterfeiting is that it is not a dream. It is a reality that continues during the reigns of Republicans and Democrats, liberals and conservatives. Inflation is not some small governmental error but counterfeiting on a grand scale. For the private individual the practice of printing bogus, worthless paper and putting it in circulation is a criminal act, yet it is legal for governments to do it. The practice of inflating the money supply with fiat currency is an act of national theft.

The reality of American counterfeiting is reflected in shrinking savings accounts, higher interest rates, lower capital investment, and higher prices. This is not the result of one greedy butcher, nor of one million greedy butchers, but rather of a government that wants to spend and is afraid to increase taxes. The two primary means of income for the government are taxes and creating money out of thin air. The latter is merely a disguised form of taxation. Inflation costs the people dearly, but the costs are hidden, at least until the taxpayer sees the results of higher prices.

During the 1980 election campaign, inflation was a central issue. Gerald Ford's WIN campaign didn't, and inflation reached double digits during the Carter administration. This aroused the public although most people did not fully understand the complexities of the issue. What people did understand was that the purchasing power of their dollar had shrunk. And the pain in their pocketbooks produced a howl in the polling booth.

In a 1983 Gallup poll, only 5 percent of the people indicated that inflation was a concern for them in the next presidential election. In the short space of three years, the problem of inflation had been solved. A miracle of Reaganomics! The inflation rate had dropped to between 3 and 4 percent. The central issues were now high interest rates and severe unemployment. A clamor arose for job programs, for government to provide funds for relief to those suffering from unemployment. With an annual deficit approaching $200 billion, the public cried for more government spending to solve the present woes of unemployment.

What causes inflation? The proximate answer is those monetary policies allowing the government to print fiat currency. But why are governments induced to use such practices? A deficit does not necessitate fiat currency, and printing money is only one alternative. Other measures can be used to overcome deficits. The government can reduce its spending or it can raise taxes. No law of causality says deficits cause inflation, but oh, the temptation on public officials to roll the presses in light of the other options.

Consider the politician's choice. He can choose to cut federal spending. Imagine the national crises that would follow a sudden reduction of government spending of $200 billion. Masses of government employees would be out of work. Entitlement and welfare programs would be seriously curtailed. Private interest groups would be furious. Very possibly there would be blood in the streets as those who suffered losses of government benefits would rise up in angry revolt. Cutting spending means losing votes. The politician can vote to increase taxes. Political historians argue that people become revolutionary if their taxes reach a certain level. That level has already doubled in the United States, and governments fear (rightly) that to meet the deficits by significant increases in taxes would be political suicide. They prefer policies of economic suicide to the political variety.

Or the politician can inflate the money supply. By increasing the money supply the government gains certain advantages. It can pay its debts with devalued currency. (Debtors benefit from inflation while creditors suffer.) Second, it is difficult to place blame. There is no voting going on. Inflation is still seen by most voters as a sin of business. However, sooner or later these inflationary monetary policies create a public furor. But this solution is simple because the public is easily deceived. The printing presses can be turned on or off, depending on the public mood.

It is relatively easy to manipulate inflation. As Milton Friedman has suggested, it only requires pushing a button to stop or start the presses. Stop the presses and you get recession with unemployment. Start the presses and you get higher prices, a loss of investment capital, a decline in production, and failing businesses. The public will probably not catch on because of the time lapse between inflating the money supply and reaping the economic consequences. During the time lapse, if the machines are shut off, the inflation rate will drop. Then the nation lives out the consequences of the earlier inflation. During this consequence period, the public looks at the visible branches but forgets the root. Suddenly unemployment becomes the issue. Inflation remains a concern of only 5 percent of the population. The government responds by spending more money and enlarging the deficit to "meet the needs of the people." This, of course, increases the temptation to turn the presses on again for a new cycle. Such a policy is as effective as extinguishing fire by pouring gasoline on it. The real causes of economic woes are obscured by the pressures of the immediate. The urgent becomes a tyrant, forcing the politician to choose the expedient rather than the prudent, because the public demands it.

A Look Back

The Wall Street crash of 1929 was a frightening experience. Survivors of the Great Depression tell tales of living through it with the pride of those who had landed on Omaha Beach on D-day. The economic upheaval was like none other. There had been previous depressions, all preceded by a period of inflation. But these depressions had come and gone quickly, as the politicians of the day wisely assumed a hands-off, laissez-faire attitude toward the economy and let it straighten itself out.

Herbert Hoover took a different approach. He undertook a campaign of increased government spending to stimulate the economy. By the standards of the time, the program was one of immense proportions. (It was only after the even greater spending plans of succeeding presidents that Hoover acquired his reputation as a fiscal conservative.) Hoover's meddling, of course, brought predictable results: The economy grew worse. And the worse things got, the more Hoover intervened.

The 1932 presidential campaign pitted Hoover, the fiscal liberal, against Franklin D. Roosevelt, the conservative. The Democratic economic platform read:

We advocate:
1. An immediate and drastic reduction of governmental expenditures by abolishing useless commissions and offices, consolidating departments and bureaus and eliminating extravagance, to accomplish a saving of not less than 25 percent in the cost of federal government.
2. Maintenance of the national credit by a federal budget annually balanced.
3. A sound currency to be maintained at all hazards.[1]

The American people were not economic illiterates. They understood, as their forefathers had, the value of limited government. Once in office Roosevelt took up the task of ending the Depression. In his inaugural address, the president stated that he wished to keep a proper balance between the executive and legislative branches of the government. He added that should Congress be lax in dealing with the Depression, he would ask Congress for more power. Americans breathed a sigh of relief as finally they had a man dedicated to fiscal sanity and limited government.

Then Roosevelt burned the party's platform and fanned the flame with his copy of Keynes's General Theory. The depressions had happened because business was slow. Business was slow because people were not buying things. The solution was to encourage consumer spending through taxation, redistribution, and inflation. Taxation, redistribution, and inflation became Roosevelt's platform. An act of Congress allowed the president to follow through on his platform. Congress declared, "All acts of the President and the Secretary of the Treasury since March 4th, 1933, are hereby confirmed and approved."

Roosevelt went to work on his new platform armed with a congressional rubber stamp. His national bank holiday took place for the purpose of finding those banks that were stable and unstable. It also enabled him to discover who owned gold, and how much. The president decreed that all persons and corporations must hand over all gold holdings or face fines and imprisonment. The American people assumed that this action was necessary for the nation's credit and that, once the crisis was over, they would redeem their paper dollars for gold. Nothing was said about devaluing the dollar or going off the gold standard. Attached to the Emergency Farm Relief Act was the Inflation Amendment. This amendment enabled the president to use $3 billion at his own discretion, and it gave him the power to devalue the dollar by one-half. The government became an ever larger operation. Spending plans and redistribution programs of all kinds cropped up. Occasionally the Supreme Court reminded Roosevelt of his constitutional obligations, but his plan rolled along virtually unhindered.

Roosevelt quietly repudiated the gold standard. New laws permitted the government to pay its debts in any kind of money, and all debts, including private ones, could be paid for in paper. Whereas old congressional records explained the words "legal tender" with "Debts may be paid in this currency," Roosevelt's repudiation of the gold standard now meant debts *must* be paid in this currency. Trade using gold was forbidden. America now had a money based on paper. The president himself declared each day the exchange rate of paper dollars to gold. Rumors spread that his decisions were often made with the rolling of dice.

The price of gold inched up slowly as Roosevelt tried to put America to work and keep the printing presses working day and night. The Depression dragged on as Roosevelt surpassed his predecessor in interference and in government spending. The American people stood in bread lines, but forgot the promises their president had made and elected him leader once more. Roosevelt offered more interference and more tampering. The gold standard had become a story for history books. Inflation was now the green light of the future.

During the regime of President Carter, the nightly news kept us posted on the price of gold as well as on the exchange rates of dollars to various foreign currencies enjoying a higher degree of stability than our own. The dollar fell steadily, day after day, in relation to gold and to foreign currencies. The nation began to worry. The inflation rate neared 20 percent. Gold climbed over the eight-hundred-dollars-an-ounce mark. Fewer than thirty years before, gold could have been bought for one-twentieth of that. Inflation was hitting the country hard.

International Consequences

Inflation has the same effect on international trade as it does on lenders. Wary of receiving devalued dollars, foreign businesses shy away from trade with America. Unstable currencies frighten everyone away. Inflated dollars are like hot potatoes—no one wants to be caught holding them.

International trade between two countries off the gold standard is dangerous business. No one knows just exactly how much another's system has been inflated. That is why exchange rates fluctuate so quickly. In a gold-based world money system, exchange rates are figured in terms of gold, and they do not change. Such a stable atmosphere is more open to international trade and thus to international mutual profit. Inflation makes international trade hazardous, taking away greater opportunities for profit. Inflation discourages international consumer spending, a Keynesian horror and a mercantilist's delight. The volume of international trade in nations with highly devalued currency is a pittance when measured against the volume of trade in countries with relatively stable currencies.

When any country goes through a period of devaluation, its currency held in foreign countries tends to return to the home country. Just as Americans do not want their money sitting in banks and losing its value, foreigners do not want to hold American money while its value shrinks. As a result, American dollars are returned to America quickly, invoking still more inflation and devaluation as the money supply grows.

Inflation hurts international trade much the same way it hurts domestic trade. A feeling of distrust toward the currency encourages foreign companies to take their business elsewhere. This loss of trade translates into a loss of profit, the first item in our list of non-negotiables for material prosperity. As inflation encourages the return of American dollars from other countries, devaluation and distrust increase. Foreigners can simply trade for their native currency and watch the value of the once strong American dollar fall.

Judgment

I do not rest my case against inflation solely on natural economic laws or on our God-given power of reason. I am not concerned solely over the lost value of my bank account or over the departure from the ideas of Adam Smith, the father of economics. I do not write as an anachronistic, "gold-bug" prophet. I am not an old Republican looking under every rock to find some dirt to throw on Franklin Delano Roosevelt.

My concern comes as a Christian concern, not in some vague sense of stewardship or a drive to build the kingdom of God but in the violation of the law of God. Just as a man who attempts to break God's law of gravity by stepping off the top of a skyscraper will fall to his death, so also will a nation pay dearly for violating God's economic laws. Our economic problems today are not based on some natural boom and bust cycle, but they have their root in lawlessness, the lawlessness of an ever-tampering, ever-hampering, ever-inflating, overgrowing government. Economic predictions are easy: As long as the government interferes in the marketplace, one can expect economic problems. When the government backs away from the market, only then will we experience economic growth and well-being.

Inflation is not merely a violation of God's general law; it bears the judgment of God in Scripture. Just as false weights and measures are forbidden in the marketplace, so also are they forbidden to the government. The use of false weights and measures in the Old Testament was an act of devaluation, an act of stealing value from another. Inflation is also an act of devaluation.

The dollar today is not the dollar of ten years ago. Neither is a quarter what it used to be. Look at the side of any quarter. The Oreo design is not for decoration; it is the intrusion of cheap metals into our coins. The government that can produce a quarter for five cents turns quite a profit. The cheaper the metals, the more profit the government makes. The American government is weighing our money with smaller and smaller stones, day by day. That same judgment on the dishonest trader of the Old Testament stands on our government today. Dross is the Old Testament word describing the impurities added to coins. Just as the impurities of our hearts cannot escape the eye of God, so also the impurities of coins do not escape his eye and judgment.

In the first chapter of the Book of Isaiah, God declares his judgment upon his chosen race. Isaiah lists many of their sins. One of them is the devaluation of coinage. "How is the faithful city become an harlot! it was full of judgment; righteousness lodged in it; but now murderers. Thy silver is become dross, thy wine mixed with water: Thy princes are rebellious, and companions of thieves: every one loveth gifts, and followeth after rewards: they judge not the fatherless, neither doth the cause of the widow come unto them" (Isa. 1:21–23). Isaiah is not telling Israel that their silver has miraculously changed to worthless dross. He is bringing an indictment from the mouth of God against this inflation. Inflation is a transgression against a righteous God.

Former president Jimmy Carter once graced the cover of a widely read, national evangelical magazine under the title of his book, *Keeping Faith*. In both the book and the magazine, Carter discussed his spiritual struggles in office and his reliance on the strength of Christ. Did Mr. Carter ever read Isaiah 1? His administration printed more paper dollars than any administration before its time. A judgment of charity demands that this policy was practiced in ignorance, yet it remains an immoral policy.

There has been little moral outrage about the systematic debasing of currency in the United States. Coalitions form to fight racism, sexism, violence on television, pornography, pollution, extinction, nuclear wars, any wars, creedism, fascism, and communism. Where is the People's Anti-Inflation Network? Why are the prudent savers in our country not marching on Washington demanding an end to the devaluation of our money? Perhaps we Christians think we should not be concerned about base, materialistic subjects such as money.

Perhaps we should be concerned with more spiritual matters. But sin is a spiritual matter, and inflation is sin.

The Tax

Jimmy Carter once said that inflation is the cruelest tax of all. It is one form of taxation that is not graduated. The minimum wage laborer loses the value of his money at the same rate as a million-dollar-a-year star athlete. Inflation knows no classes or tax brackets; it robs indiscriminately. Yet the hardest hit are the poor and the elderly with fixed incomes.

Taxation is the money the government takes from individuals. This is what politicians are forced to keep down. Inflation, however, allows the politician to promise government financial support to every cause and its corollary. Inflation is a blank check, covered and insured only by the printing press. But inflation, the printing of fiat money, diminishes purchasing power. Through inflation, the government takes away the value of the money that remains in your hands after taxation. The government taxes your purchasing power by flooding the marketplace with crisp new counterfeit bills. This too is taxation, the kind that is not mentioned in campaign speeches. This taxation doesn't show up under "withheld"; it shows up in higher prices around the country where businessmen rather than politicians take the blame. Our dollars do not actually shrink; their purchasing power shrinks. The connection is indirect but real and this tax is silent as well as devastating.

It is also covert, carried on behind the closed doors of government. No one announces that the government will take a given percentage of the consumer's purchasing power during the next fiscal year. No one announces just how much the government's fiscal policies will cost your savings account. The American people remain in an economic slumber as their money loses value day by day. Despite the rhetoric from our presidents, red ink appears on the budget year after year. The dollar inflates as its purchasing power declines. Nixon tried price controls; Carter tried guidelines. Yet the budget still does not balance, and the presses keep printing. The unemployment lines, the shutdown factories, and higher bills are only the beginning of the inevitable economic collapse brought on by inflation. Where is Isaiah?

We have discussed the havoc inflation plays with capital investment. Shrinking savings accounts and high inflationary risk drive up interest rates, making investment in new tools of production difficult and often impossible. Not only does this lack of investment hit the executive in his wallet, it forces the continuance of poverty. While businessmen in tailored suits sit in leather chairs discussing the theoretical difficulties of inflation, the new immigrant sits in his dimly lit, one-room apartment, unemployed. Why? Because he lives in an economy stagnant from lack of investment. And this lack of investment stems from the many, paper fiat dollars in our system. The futility of saving hits both the poor man and the rich man. However, the poor man pays for both his own and the rich man's inability to save. The rich man cannot save and therefore he cannot invest. Since he is unable to invest, his business cannot grow, and he cannot hire more workers. And that is why the poor man sits in his slum, unemployed.

Inflation torpedoes material prosperity. In an inflated economy, saving is foolish. However, we cannot enjoy material well-being without savings. The work ethic does not say, Work hard and you'll go places, but rather, Work hard, save, and you'll go places. If one doesn't save, he can go nowhere. If one does save, but his money is losing its value to inflation, he can go nowhere. Breaking the prosperity cycle affects people of all economic levels, from the multimillionaire to the low-skilled laborer. But it is the poor who bear the brunt of its evils. They have no back-up resources and, if they cannot find work, they cannot provide for themselves and their families.

The Benefit

If inflation creates this multitude of problems, why do we permit it? Who is benefiting from it? The politicians who live off the ignorance of the populace. They are able to promise endless programs, take full credit, and place the blame on someone else. They promise more money for the home state and lower taxes, and they blame the deficit on anything from defense spending to the length of women's skirts. The charade continues year after year.

Those who benefit the most from inflation are those on the government payroll—defense contractors, public employees, federal relief recipients, social security recipients, the countless millions who at one time or another receive a check from the federal government. These people receive the inflated money first before its value has had a chance to go down. This fiat money is passed on until it reaches the lowest echelons, the poor who are least aware of the complexities of economics.

Inflation benefits the wheeling-dealing politicians of our day by giving them the power to buy votes, literally. Every federal program, from low-cost housing to sewage systems to defense factories to power plants such as the Tennessee Valley Authority, comes via the courtesy of inflation. Every raised price, every increase in the interest rate, every devaluation of savings comes ultimately from the Bureau of Engraving and Printing.

Conclusion

Inflation is not higher prices. It is an increase in the money supply. The responsibility for inflation rests solely in the hands of government, the federal government. Inflation is not the scheme of a butcher hoping for a second car; it is the scheme of countless government officials hoping for a second term.

Inflation is an exercise in the production of fiat money. The dictionary defines fiat money as paper money decreed legal tender, not backed by gold or silver and not necessarily redeemable in coin.[2] This is an apt description of our American dollar. Our money is fiat money backed by order of the government and nothing else. The government's declaration that green paper is money is akin to my declaring my dog a cat. Surely I have the authority to do this, inasmuch as the dog belongs to me; but I do not have the power. Neither does the government have the power to make paper have real value.

The government stands guilty of breaking its own laws. It has set itself above the law in this act of counterfeiting. The Federal Reserve, the president, and the legislature all take part in this. Perhaps the law against counterfeiting exists only to protect the government, to insure a monopoly in printing money.

The government not only forbids any other form of money (for example, real money like gold or silver), but legal tender laws now prevent the use of anything but devalued paper and devalued coins issued by the government in any trade transactions. Trade in America now takes place only with the medium of exchange dictated by the government, government fiat money and nothing else. The government protects itself on all sides.

If we are to stop the unethical and economically destructive use of inflation as a tool of government interventionism, we must do more than turn off the money machine. As long as the government has the legal power to use this machine, the odds are that the "on" switch will be pressed again. This is especially likely if the federal deficit continues to swell and budgets continue to go unbalanced. We must either destroy the machine or limit it to printing money with hard value behind it. As long as no law requires that our paper currency be backed by hard money of some sort, the government has the legal right to counterfeit.

Seven

Biblical Concern for the Poor

The word "poor" functions as more than a working definition for a group of people lacking material goods. Not only is poor a descriptive term; it is an emotive term, one that provokes feelings ranging from compassion to fury. The mere mention of the poor can inspire political zeal or sound a rallying cry for revolution. On the lips of a demagogue it becomes a cry for political action. On the lips of an elitist it turns into a contemptuous epithet. So much unspoken and undefined excess baggage accompanies the phrase that it begs for more sober qualification.

Who are the poor? Why are they poor? What does it mean to be poor? If we are to cut through the emotions and penetrate to the substantive, we need a clear definition and a basic understanding of the root causes of poverty.

Poor is a relative term that assumes some standard of wealth. Poverty levels are adjusted from culture to culture, from generation to generation, even from year to year. The current poverty level of income would have placed a family in the upper middle class in 1900 and in the middle class in 1950. As the purchasing power of the dollar fluctuates, so does the poverty level. Even if we defined poor as a lack of material goods, we would still face the problem of relativity. A person living in the United States today without benefit of indoor plumbing or electricity might easily be called poor. Yet little more than a century ago, even the upper class used outhouses and candles.

To clarify the meaning of the term, we must reach beyond such cultural relativities and define those essentials the poor lack, either entirely or in part. We may include such necessities as food, clothing, shelter, and health care, and we may add to these with education, transportation, tools of production, and other material benefits. Are we speaking of people who are starving to death for lack of food or freezing to death for lack of clothing and shelter? Are we talking about those who lack educational opportunity, sophisticated tools, or modern means of transportation? A native islander may be well fed, adequately clothed and housed, yet still be using a mule instead of a tractor. He may have the bare necessities of life, indeed he may have the riches of a tribal chieftain, yet still be poor in terms of worldwide standards of living.

We see then that poverty is not an absolute. It is better defined in terms of a continuum with two poles ranging from extreme poverty, where even the bare necessities of life are lacking, through a midpoint of reasonable comfort to the opposite pole of opulent luxury. As long as one person exists who lacks something another enjoys, we can speak of a relative continuum. Unless all wealth was to be distributed absolutely equally, the terms "rich" and "poor" remain relative terms.

Jesus' statement, "Ye have the poor always with you" (Matt. 26:11), does not mean we can't do anything about poverty nor does it indicate Jesus was unconcerned about the plight of the poor. His statement was not passive resignation to an unalterable human dilemma. Jesus' life was a portrait of energetic ministry to the poor, and his ethic was one of compassionate concern for the poor. The fact that the poor are always with us is not a license for indifference but a call to long-term ministry.

I once spoke to a minister who had devoted thirty years of daily ministry to the urban poor in Cleveland, Ohio. I asked him how he endured the daily frustrations of his ministry over three decades. He replied, "I take comfort in Jesus' words, 'The poor you always have with you.' Many of my young assistants have grown disillusioned and bitter after two or three years. Their idealism has been shattered when their seminary dreams of eliminating poverty have not been quickly realized. My job is not to eliminate poverty but to bring the compassion of Christ to bear on it every day." This minister was doing more than giving alms; he was attacking the root causes of poverty in his neighborhood. He was working relentlessly toward the elimination of poverty, knowing full well that however much progress he achieved, he would not be able to eliminate poverty altogether.

Kinds of Poverty

In the Old Testament, just treatment in the law courts is of primary importance to concern for the poor. Yehezkel Kaufmann in his important work, *The Religion of Israel,* maintains:

> Every Israelite is enjoined from showing partiality, taking bribes, and perverting justice (Exod. 23:3, 7ff; Lev. 19:15, 35). The duty of dealing rightly with the poor and the helpless is emphasized (Exod. 23:6; Deut. 24:17; 27:19); God himself is the model in biblical justice. Israelite law—as distinct from other Near Eastern law—recognizes no class privileges.[1]

In Israel, justice was to keep her blindfold on; she was not allowed to peek. The guiding principle was no partiality before the bar of justice.

Not only was it forbidden to grant special favors to the rich and powerful, it was also forbidden to give the poor special treatment. "Do not show favoritism to a poor man in his law-suit" (Exod. 23:3 NIV). Leviticus 19:15 states the law succinctly: "Thou shalt not respect the person of the poor, nor honour the person of the mighty: but in righteousness shalt thou judge thy neighbour." The curse of God falls upon those who take advantage of the weak or helpless in the courtroom (Deut. 27:19).

Israel had no provision for lobby groups or special-interest groups. The principle was rule by law, not rule by men. Just laws of impartiality were sacrosanct. They were not to be changed or repealed, whether by the whims of malevolent tyrants or by the self-serving interests of a voting majority.

Karl Marx complained that laws in capitalistic societies tend to reflect the vested interests of the ruling classes. The rich and powerful will, according to Marx, ultimately influence legislation to give themselves an edge in economic competition. Yet de Tocqueville warned that the edge can be gained by either side. The powerful will influence legislation, but the powerful are not always the rich. The political power of large voting blocs can offset the individual power of a single wealthy individual. In a society where the majority rules, the majority can exercise a tyranny over the minority. De Tocqueville's warning that the democratic experiment of the United States may be destroyed "when the people discover that they can vote themselves largesse" is already a fulfilled prophecy. (The graduated income tax, for example, is a glaring indication that partiality is shown to the poor.) Those in the higher income brackets represent a powerless minority who are becoming victims of economic injustice.

To deal effectively and properly with poverty, we must first distinguish different kinds of poverty. The Bible mentions four different causes of poverty, each demanding a different response from the Christian. We must understand these distinctions if we wish to ameliorate the problem. They are slothfulness, calamity, exploitation, and personal sacrifice. To lump these four groups together, seeking a common solution, is as foolish as trying to cure cancer, heart disease, the common cold, and insomnia with one pill. So let us examine each one separately.

Slothfulness

The Bible clearly speaks out against those who are poor because they are lazy. Laziness is a real and serious human problem. Karl Barth listed sloth as one of the primary and foundational sins of man, along with pride and dishonesty. According to Barth, this triad of vices constitutes the root causes of all other sins.[2]

Slothfulness involves a refusal to fulfill God's creation mandate to work, and God comes down hard on it. "Go to the ant, thou sluggard; consider her ways, and be wise" (Prov. 6:6). It is a pitiful and sinful man who must look to insects for instruction. God commands hard work from his people, and this is a command both the wealthy and the poor dare not overlook.

Paul speaks about the slothful poor when he writes, "If any would not work, neither should he eat" (2 Thess. 3:10). Biblical compassion is limited by the demand for work. The lazy have only themselves to blame for their poverty and will be required to answer for it before our holy God. Slothfulness must not be indulged by the Christian community.

It is difficult to be lazy and not poor, but it is possible to be poor and not lazy. Understanding this principle is crucial if we are to withstand the temptation of reducing all poverty to the single cause of slothfulness. It would be convenient to assume that the only cause for poverty is slothfulness. If this were so, we could be justified in closing our ears to the poor, leaving them to their just deserts. Sloth is one cause of poverty, but by no means the only cause.

Calamity

The Scripture also recognizes that many are made poor by calamity: the man born blind, the person left crippled by an accident, the farmer whose crops have been destroyed by flood or drought—all have just cause for their impoverished state.

Let us use Job as our example. Job was a hardworking, God-fearing, wealthy man. Tragedy struck again and again, leaving him a broken man. His friends ran to his side, not to show compassion or to help but to accuse Job of deplorable sins.

The Lord allows rain to fall on the fields of the good and the bad, and he likewise allows floods to cover the fields of the wicked and the righteous (see Matt. 5:45). We cannot determine the secret counsel of God in these events but we are called to respond to God's revealed commands to assist the victims of disaster and we will be held accountable before God for how we react. To these victims, we are to show compassion and genuine charity. It is the responsibility of God's people to see to it that the suffering of these people is ameliorated. They are to be a priority concern of the church. They are the hungry to be fed, the naked to be clothed (see Matt. 25:31–46). We must care for those people struck by calamities.

Exploitation

This group of poor suffers indignities by living in societies where the social, political, and judicial institutions favor the rich and powerful and leave the poor without advocacy. One such society was Israel in the eighth century B.C., when "the poor were sold for a pair of shoes." Another was apartheid in

South Africa. The government there outlawed equitable treatment of blacks by business, and certainly refused them justice. This kind of oppression provokes God, who hears the moans of his people. Such injustice should likewise move the church to legitimate social action.

Personal Sacrifice

Finally, some are poor as the result of personal sacrifice. In the New Testament, these are referred to as "the poor for righteousness' sake." This group is comprised of people who are poor voluntarily, as a result of conscious decisions to choose lifestyles or vocations with little or no financial remuneration. They are poor because their priorities do not mesh with the value standards of the culture in which they live. This group includes people such as Martin Luther, who passed up a promising and lucrative career to wear a monk's habit, and the modern businessman who passes up the windfall deal because he has scruples about hidden unethical elements. God promises special blessings to this class of poor.

The distinctions between these four kinds of poverty are essential. We must not succumb to the tendency to generalize or lump the poor together in one package. At the same time, we must avoid the equally dangerous temptation of grouping the rich. It would be unjust and slanderous to maintain that all rich people are corrupt, as if all riches were achieved through evil means or through exploiting the poor. (Take Abraham, Job, David, and Joseph of Arimathea as examples.)

We must recognize that God cares deeply about human poverty, and our duty as Christians is to be no less concerned than God himself. As long as the poor are with us, we are called to minister to them, not only through charity, but by seeking and working for the reformation of social and political structures that enslave, oppress, and exploit them.

The Biblical Response

The Bible sets down laws for dealing with the poor and offers us a way of dealing with poverty that is far greater than any elaborate Great Society scheme. It calls us to personal, concrete action.

Scripture demands our attention on widows and orphans. Exodus 22:22–24 reads: "Ye shall not afflict any widow, or fatherless child. If thou afflict them in any wise, and they cry at all unto me, I will surely hear their cry; and my wrath shall wax hot, and I will kill you with the sword; and your wives shall be widows, and your children fatherless." Dealing with these oppressed people is a core obligation of our religion. James 1:27 reads, "Pure religion and undefiled before God and the Father is this, To visit the fatherless and widows in their affliction, and to keep himself unspotted from the world."

Paul told Timothy to "honor widows" (1 Tim. 5:3). The Greek word translated "honor" is often used in Scripture to indicate payment, and it is obviously used in that manner here. Paul does, however, set limits on giving to widows. Regular support must be given only to those who are truly widows, too old to remarry, and without family, thus unable to receive support from relatives. But the restrictions run deeper. Only the widow who is engaged in charitable service is eligible to receive the church's support. She must be "well known for her good deeds, such as bringing up children, showing hospitality, washing the feet of the saints, helping those in trouble and devoting herself to all kinds of good deeds" (1 Tim. 5:10 NIV). Biblical charity does not subsidize the slothful.

The chain of responsibility in dealing with poverty is simple. The Bible calls for responsible action by both families and individuals. First in line comes the family. The second scout is the church, taking over the responsibility if there is no family.

Auberon Herbert said more than a century ago:

So long as great government departments . . . supply our wants, so long shall we remain in our present condition, the difficulties of life unconquered, and ourselves unfitted to conquer them. No amount of state education will make a really intelligent nation; no amount of Poor Laws will place a nation above want; no amount of Factory Acts will make us better parents. These great wants which we are now vainly trying to deal with by acts of Parliament, by prohibitions and penalties, are in truth the great occasions of progress, if only we surmount them by developing in ourselves more active desires, by putting forth greater efforts, by calling new moral forces into existence, and by perfecting our national ability for acting together in voluntary associations. To have our wants supplied from without by a huge state machinery, to be regulated and inspected by great armies of officials, who are themselves slaves to the system which they administer, will in the long run teach us nothing, will profit us nothing.[3]

Christian giving is not the impersonal, computerized distribution of wealth. Christian giving is personal care, the kind that lovingly encourages the recipients to get back on their feet again soon. Our goal as Christians should not be to make sure the poor are fed, but rather to insure that they are fed through biblical means.

God wants to build responsible relationships within families. Paul writes to Timothy, "If any provide not for his own, and specially for those of his own house, he hath denied the faith, and is worse than an infidel" (1 Tim. 5:8). Paul did not write, "If anyone does not see to it that his own are provided for." A man must provide for his family—his parents and all relatives who need him. He is not to pass the responsibility on to the government, even though it is surely better equipped because it holds the power of taxation. It is the man's job, and he is "worse than an infidel" if he does not do it. These are strong words, words we dare not overlook.

The family holds first responsibility in caring for the poor. However, there are poor without family and poor without responsible family. In such cases, the church bears the responsibility for their care. But we must remember that the church is not merely the organized institution of the worshiping assembly—it is the people of God.

Tithing

Old Testament Israel had a system of not one tithe, but three. The first tithe went to the Levites. Levites were not just official priests, they were also teachers, musicians, judges, and physicians. Most of the tithe, in fact, went to those who were not priests. This illustrates a principle for today: all of our tithe need not go directly to the church; other institutions need our financial support too. It may go to a Christian educational organization, a Christian hospital, or Christian missions. Building the kingdom of God, like building a successful business, requires investment capital, and this requires our tithes.

The second tithe, another 10 percent of increase, was used for a yearly festival gathering. One tenth of a family's income was to be spent having a party. Deuteronomy 14:26 reads, "And thou shalt bestow that money for whatsoever thy soul lusteth after, for oxen, or for sheep, or for wine, or for strong drink, or for whatsoever thy soul desireth: and thou shalt eat there before the LORD thy God, and thou shalt rejoice, thou, and thine household." This is a far cry from any Manichaean ideal of abstinence from physical pleasures. God calls us to rejoice in the abundance that comes from his blessing. Other cultures in the days of ancient Israel suffered famine and starvation, but Israel was called to celebrate its bounty. God commanded that one tenth of Israel's income go toward this celebration of thanksgiving to God, the giver of material prosperity.

The third tithe was not annual, but was offered in the third and sixth years of every seven-year cycle. This tithe, known as the poor tithe, was used to feed the Levites, strangers, widows, and orphans who lived in the community. This tithe, though used only two years out of every seven, was not a substitute for the first or second tithe. It was separate but as binding as the first two (Deut. 14:20–29).

Note that the Levites were included in this tithe. They were not recipients due to their state of poverty. On the contrary, they were generally the wealthiest group in Israelite society. The Levites received benefits from all three tithes as a visual sign of the importance of God's law in society and of the necessity to further his Word in every area. The Old Testament model knows nothing of the modern ideal of keeping the clergy and other administrators of God's Word poor and humble.

The poor tithe was administered locally and personally. This is significant in light of our present-day problems of red tape and bureaucracy in dealing with the poor. Individual families in Israel, those paying the poor tithe, were required to have personal contact with the poor in their communities. This contact kept well-to-do Israelites aware of the condition of the poor, and it ensured that money was given to those who were truly in need. Poverty, for most Americans, is as distant as a big-city ghetto or the highlands of the Kentucky Appalachians. We soothe our consciences by writing checks, but we stay clear of meeting poverty face-to-face. Old Testament Israel had to face the poor; it had to see their conditions and become personally involved in their care.

This poor tithe also had safeguards against supporting irresponsibility. The poor tithe was collected only two years in seven. A poor man could not count on a continuous supply of free food. God showed mercy on the poor by commanding charity to them and by keeping the wealthy aware of their plight, but the poor did not have a running claim on the beneficence of the rich. The wealthy were responsible to contribute the poor tithe, and the poor were also responsible to contribute the poor tithe. The poor were responsible for finding gainful employment as well, to pull themselves out of poverty and become productive citizens of God's kingdom. The principle that Paul later stated also applied in Old Testament Israel: If a man wouldn't work, he couldn't eat. The poor laws were not designed to subsidize poverty.

Murray Rothbard, in his voluminous work *Man, Economy, and State,* writes:

> State poor relief is clearly a subsidization of poverty, for men are now automatically entitled to money from the state because of their poverty. Hence, the marginal disutility of income fore-gone from leisure diminishes, and idleness and poverty tend to increase further, which in turn increases the amount of sub-sidy that must be extracted from the taxpayers. Thus, a sys-tem of legally subsidized poverty tends to call forth more of the very poverty that is supposedly being alleviated. A man will not work if he is assured of minimal comforts not work-ing. The reason to work is simply not there as a man today can be paid by the government to not work.[4]

God's system avoids this problem by making it economically desirable to work one's way out of poverty. Rothbard writes on private charity: "Private charity to the poor, on the other hand, would not have the same vicious-circle effect, since the poor would not have a continuing compulsory claim on the rich. This is particularly true where private charity is given only to the 'deserving' poor."[5] Under the biblical poor laws, the vicious cir-cle is avoided. Poverty is neither subsidized nor ignored.

Gleaning

Gleaning was the only charity the poor of Israel regularly received. Farmers were forbidden to harvest the corners of their fields, and fruit remaining after the trees had been beaten and shaken stayed there for the poor to pick. Leviticus 19:9–10 reads:

> And when ye reap the harvest of your land, thou shalt not wholly reap the corners of thy field, neither shalt thou gather the glean-

ings of thy harvest. And thou shalt not glean thy vineyard, neither shalt thou gather every grape of thy vineyard; thou shalt leave them for the poor and stranger: I am the LORD your God.

Deuteronomy 24:19–22 further elaborates:

When thou cuttest down thine harvest in thy field, and hast forgot a sheaf in the field, thou shalt not go again to fetch it: it shall be for the stranger, for the fatherless, and for the widow: that the LORD thy God may bless thee in all the work of thine hands. When thou beatest thine olive tree, thou shalt not go over the boughs again: it shall be for the stranger, for the fatherless, and for the widow. When thou gatherest the grapes of thy vineyard, thou shalt not glean it afterward: it shall be for the stranger, for the fatherless, and for the widow. And thou shalt remember that thou wast a bondman in the land of Egypt: therefore I command thee to do this thing.

While gleaning laws reflected God's compassion for the poor, they did not foster irresponsibility. Gleaning did not amount to corporate ownership of land. Landowners still had the right to specify those deserving poor who could glean on their land. The story of Ruth illustrates this.

Then said Boaz unto Ruth, Hearest thou not, my daughter? Go not to glean in another field, neither go from hence, but abide here fast by my maidens: Let thine eyes be on the field that they do reap, and go thou after them: have I not charged the young men that they shall not touch thee? and when thou art athirst, go unto the vessels, and drink of that which the young men have drawn.

Ruth 2:8–9

Ruth did not simply claim her right to glean, but bowed to the ground in appreciation of the generosity and compassion of Boaz. The responsibility of feeding the poor rested on the shoulders of the citizens of Israel, not upon the government. The poor had no legal claim to the fruit of the farmer's labor, yet they were fed.

Another aspect of gleaning differs greatly from our present system. Gleaning was hard work, unlike running to one's mailbox to receive a government check. It was harder work than harvesting. The corners of fields quite often lay in heavy thicket, and the fruits that remained were few, hard to find, and still harder to pick. The poor could be fed through gleaning, but it was to one's advantage to find gainful employment. Lazy poor were not fed nor were they invited to glean. This biblical plan of charity nurtured responsibility rather than welfare fraud, hereditary poverty, or generation after generation of families fed by a bureaucratic welfare system.

Eight

Equality vs. Equity

All of us, at one time or another, have had our convictions attacked. It can be a confusing and disheartening experience. A man argues with me that Jesus never rose from the dead, that his ethical teachings were naive. I do not understand why this man doubts that God has power over death nor why he doubts the Word of God on the subject of right and wrong. At the same time, he cannot understand how I can put my trust in someone he views as a desert-walking, religious fanatic.

Similar misunderstandings exist in economics. To the socialist, the capitalist is an overweight, cigar-smoking man whose only moral guide is dollars and cents. The socialist sees the conservative economist as someone who prefers a world where the haves prosper and the have-nots suffer, who defends industrial pillaging, sweatshops, child labor, and individualistic competition. The conservative looks at a socialist through equally jaundiced eyes. Socialists are caricatured as hardened revolutionaries seeking to burn our sacred Constitution, destroy our national wealth, and enslave all of us in the name of economic equality.

It is not a pretty picture, nor is it an accurate one. Vision becomes distorted when we enter the political arena. It is difficult to criticize an opponent fairly or to exercise judgment

113

in charity. It is easier to succumb to the temptation of using worst-case analysis for the other side while reserving the right of best-case analysis for ourselves. Asking a political or economic conservative to describe a liberal is like asking a Hatfield to describe a McCoy. The result is more often slander and exaggeration than accuracy.

My objective in writing this book is not to praise socialism but to bury it. I am convinced that political and economic policies involving the forced redistribution of wealth via government intervention are neither right nor safe. Such policies are both unethical and ineffective. They are not unethical because they are ineffective (the canon of moral judgment is not the slippery norm of pragmatism) but because they are wrong in principle. They violate both natural law *(lex naturalis)* and supernatural law *(lex aeternitatis)*.

None of this negates the fact that the intentions of many, if not most, of those espousing such policies are honorable. The prime motive of socialism is to help the poor. This motive is both noble and godly. God wants the poor helped. On the surface it would seem that socialists are on God's side. Unfortunately, their programs and their means foster greater poverty even though their hearts remain loyal to eliminating poverty. The tragic fallacy that invades socialist thinking is that there is a necessary, causal connection between the wealth of the wealthy and the poverty of the poor. Socialists assume that one man's wealth is based on another man's poverty; therefore, to stop poverty and help the poor man, we must have socialism.

If the motive of socialism is to help the poor, the prime goal of a socialist state is to bring about equal distribution of wealth. There is a sharp contrast between the luxury of Beverly Hills and the misery of nearby Watts. The contrast produces a sense of holy anger. It seems unjust, immoral, and unbiblical for some to live so well and for others to be so poor. Equality of wealth would mean an end to this imbalance and apparent injustice. The highest expression of social justice, according to socialist theory, is not equal treatment under the law, but equal participation in wealth.

A teacher illustrated this equation of equal justice and equal wealth in a discussion with her middle-school students. The majority of the students agreed that the wealth of our country should be divided equally. The teacher argued against this conclusion but failed to persuade the youngsters otherwise. Days later the teacher returned a test her students had taken earlier. Each student received a grade of 72.6 percent. One student, who had answered all of the questions correctly, questioned his grade. The teacher explained that another student had not done very well on the test so she gave him some of the better student's points. To ensure a fair distribution of grades, she explained, she had divided the points equally among the students. The students, of course, objected to this new system, and the teacher gently reminded them of their discussion a few days earlier.

There is a subtle but paramount distinction between equality and equity. Equality is likeness, evenness, and uniformity. Equity is justice, impartiality, and fairness. Socialism calls for equality; the Scriptures call for equity. The distinction between equality and equity is blurred whenever the righteous call to equity brings about the unholy call to material equality.

Psalm 98:9 reads, "With righteousness shall he judge the world, and the people with equity." The Bible is clear. Nowhere in the Old Testament do we find a hint of legislation designed to bring material equality, but we do find repeated warnings against inequity. Amos spoke out against unjust judges who were easily bribed, using one system of law for the rich and another for the poor. A poor man during the days of Israel's apostasy had no chance of a fair ruling from a judge. When equity could not be found, God's wrath burned. First Samuel 2:7 says, "The LORD maketh poor, and maketh rich." The Lord did not build an egalitarian society based on the equal redistribution of wealth.

The word *equality* appears two times in the New Testament. In 2 Corinthians 8:13–15, Paul asks the church at Corinth to assist financially the needy Christians in Jerusalem: "For I mean not that other men be eased, and ye burdened: but by an equality, that now at this time your abundance may be a supply for their want, that their abundance also may be a supply for your want: that there may be equality: As it is written, He that had gathered much had nothing over; and he that had gathered little had no lack."

Paul is not advocating an equal redistribution of wealth, but rather that the Corinthians voluntarily help out in a time of need in Jerusalem. Equality here is not used in an absolute leveling sense, but rather in the sense that all should have enough to eat. Philip Hughes writes:

> As Hodge points out, what Paul is advocating here "is not agrarianism, nor community of goods," for in the New Testament all giving is voluntary and the fruit of love. Its object is the relief of want, not an artificial equalization of property . . . Thus . . . the Scriptures avoid, on the one hand, the injustice and destructive evils of agrarian communism, by recognizing the right of property and making all almsgiving optional; and on the other, the heartless disregard of the poor by inculcating the universal brotherhood of believers, and the consequent duty of each to contribute of his abundance to relieve the necessities of the poor.[1]

Colossians 4:1 reads, "Masters, give unto your servants that which is just and equal." Paul is not calling for socialistic income redistribution here either. Rather he is demanding that slaveholders be responsible and insure the necessities of life for their slaves.

The principle here is fairness. The slave master is reminded that he too has a master in heaven. This is a simple application of the golden rule, not a credo for egalitarianism. J. B. Lightfoot adds: "It seems a mistake to suppose that ιτότης *(isotēs)* has anything to do with the treatment of slaves as equals (comp. Philem. 16). When connected with δίκαιον *(dikaion)*, the word naturally suggests an evenhanded, impartial treatment and is equivalent to the Latin aequitas."[2] Paul is saying, then, that a wealthy slave owner and the slave himself are equal if they both have enough to eat.

Justice

Our Declaration of Independence holds as a self-evident truth that all men are created equal. The framers of the Declaration knew full well that in the colonies some men were more wealthy than others. They did not seek to change this. Their concern was for justice, not equality of wealth. All men, poor or wealthy, farmer or merchant, deserve equal justice under the law. No man is to receive preferential treatment in the courts. Legal justice and economic equality are not the same thing. Though both involve a kind of equality, the equality has two different referents. Equality in a judicial sense is impartiality in judgment; equality of wealth is the even distribution of goods and services to all people.

Equality of material ownership may be a noble ideal in a world where sin is not present. If all people were equally industrious, equally productive, equally prudent, and equally in need, then justice might require equal distribution of wealth. But to enforce such an equality in a world where some are industrious while others are slothful, and where some are productive while others are wasteful, is not to establish justice but to destroy it. In such a system, equity is swallowed up by equality.

Advocates of a transfer society in which the power of the state is used to force a redistribution of wealth constantly couch their platforms in two noble phrases: "social justice" and "the goal of economic equality." These twin concepts are noble in intention and might work in a sinless society, but to coerce economic equality in a sinful society is to perform social injustice. The redistributionist is guilty of calling evil good. His end is noble, but his means ignoble; his goal is altruistic, but his methods are tyrannical.

The only way to have a transfer society is to violate justice. The cornerstone of most redistributionist policies is legalized theft—taking from the rich by force, and giving to the poor. If the rich had initially gained their wealth by stealing from the poor, then the return of their property would merely be restitution. But redistributionism goes well beyond restitution to egalitarian transfers couched in euphemisms like "entitlement." The advocate of authentic social justice asks, "Why am I entitled to the fruit of another man's labor? What right do I have to my neighbor's property?"

God is no respecter of persons. His character and his law are our ultimate norms for justice. The difference between equality and equity is clearly discernible in the way God deals with his people. Both the rich and the poor enter into his judgment. Both the rich and the poor are redeemed through the life, death, and resurrection of his Son, Jesus Christ. Our God is both just and merciful, yet he does not shower his material blessings on every man equally. Both Noah and Jacob divided their patriarchal blessings according to the performances of their sons. The Promised Land was not divided equally among the twelve tribes. Reward and punishment are given out according to obedience or disobedience throughout Scripture.

The crux of the debate between advocates of a free economic society and a state-dominated, transfer society lies in the definition of justice. The word "justice" has become a catchword that plays a strong, emotive role in socialist platforms, while its content dangles in an atmosphere of ambiguity. "Social justice" is a rallying cry that is left undefined.

Ronald Nash has done a careful study of the classic meaning of justice in his book, *Social Justice and the Christian*

Church. He comments on Aristotle's distinction between three kinds of justice: commercial justice, remedial justice, and distributive justice. Nash writes:

> (1) Interpersonal relations involving economic exchanges raise questions of commercial justice. When people exchange goods and services, questions arise as to whether the exchange is fair or the compensation just. Passages of Scripture like Leviticus 19:36 and Proverbs 16:11 that advise merchants to have just scales and weights seem directed to this type of justice.
>
> (2) Instances where some wrong must be made right under either criminal or civil law are occasions for remedial justice. Cases where an innocent individual is found guilty or where the punishment for an offense is too severe or too lenient are instances of injustice in this sense. Exodus 23:3–6 is one of a number of biblical passages that speak to issues of remedial justice.
>
> (3) Finally, questions about distributive justice arise in situations where some good or burden is apportioned among human beings. Such situations are encountered frequently as, for example, when a parent divides the evening dessert among the members of a large family, or a man divides his estate among his heirs. As the term is used in contemporary writing, social justice is viewed as that species of distributive justice concerned with the distribution of burdens and benefits within society as a whole, a distribution that is usually controllable by political authorities.[3]

Classical philosophers wrestled with the question of the relationship between justice and human rights. The Bible repeatedly links the term "justice" with righteousness. Justice is to be given according to righteousness. A right is made obligatory by righteousness.

The noun "right" can function in different ways. We distinguish, for example, between legal rights and moral rights. In a perfect society where the laws reflect absolute righteousness, we would expect no discrepancies between moral and legal rights. But such a society does not exist on this planet. Legislatures err, and unjust and unrighteous laws inevitably emerge.

The term "right" is so emotionally charged in our culture that it frequently functions as a subterfuge for personal preference. A personal desire is translated by linguistic sleight-of-hand into a moral imperative that must be granted by righteous obligation. Consider the raging debate in the United States on the abortion issue. One of the repeated claims of advocates of abortion on demand is that a woman has the right to control her own body. This right includes sovereignty over her own pregnancy. When this claim is made, we must ask, What kind of right does the woman have? A legal right? A moral right? If the claim is simply that a woman has a legal right to abortion and therefore, the present abortion laws ought to remain intact, then the argument is circular. It translates, I ought to have the right because I have the right. What is probably meant, however, is that a woman has a moral right to control her own body. That is, righteousness demands that a woman be free to terminate a pregnancy if she chooses. But whence cometh this moral right? If God is the ultimate norm of righteousness, a moral right is a God-given right. It is precisely at this point that the abortion advocate is in trouble. God is strangely silent about such moral rights. Indeed, unless the argument includes a defense of how righteousness demands such a right, the argument is gratuitous. As it stands, it is a mere declaration, not a reasoned argument.

Let us apply this distortion of the word "right" to the economic arena. Consider the news coverage of steelworkers converging on the corporate headquarters of U.S. Steel. The company has just announced the shut-down of another large mill with the resulting layoff of hundreds of workers. The unemployed steelworkers picket the corporate headquarters with placards proclaiming their right to remain employed. Spokesmen angrily demand that the company restore their rightful jobs. Company spokesmen defend the closing of the mill on the grounds that it is losing money. U.S. Steel, they argue, is in business to make a profit.

Does a company have the moral obligation to provide jobs if the company is losing money? Conversely, does a human being have an inalienable right to be employed and every American an intrinsic right to a job? We know that God imposes on people a moral obligation to work. Does that obligation at the same time impose an obligation on someone else to provide the job? The answer is self-evident: While I am responsible to work, my obligation does not imply either logically or morally that someone else has the obligation to employ me. Employment is a trade agreement whereby both parties profit. I sell my labor for wages. If my labor is not desired, no one has an obligation to employ me.

Then what is justice? Nash relates justice to a person's due:

The ancients believed that justice always involves giving a person his due, that to which he has a right. The reason why a person may be due something varies with his or her situation. A hypothetical person named Jones would be due something in each of the following cases:

(1) If Jones does better work than any other student in the class, she is due the best grade.
(2) If Jones is the prettiest contestant in a beauty contest, she is due first prize.
(3) If Jones is the first to finish a race, she is due the prize.
(4) If Jones is promised something by Smith, Jones is due the fulfillment of that promise.
(5) If Jones' property is stolen or damaged by Smith, Jones is due whatever reparation is required to restore what she lost.

The what and the why of any person's due cannot be reduced to a single formula. . . . However much of the determination of a person's due varies with the situation, it seems clear that the essence of justice involves each person having or receiving that which he is due. At the very least, justice occurs in situations where people receive what he or she is due. In any case where someone is denied what he or she is due, an injustice has occurred.[4]

Socialism distorts justice. The fruits of one man's labor are given to another in the interest of equality and at the expense of equity. The poor man is assumed to have the right to the wealth of another man. The wealthy man loses his right to the fruit of his own labor. Under a socialist economy the poor are not lifted up in order to produce equality, the wealthy are brought down. Socialism breeds an unjust bias against the wealthy, making them the target of public scorn and inequitable taxation.

It is difficult to generate sympathy for the wealthy. Their wealth provides them with so many advantages, so many luxuries, so much power, that it is easy for the envious to assume the rich can afford injustice. Media images frequently depict the rich as unscrupulous, pompous, foolish, wasteful, bigoted, and uncaring. The J. R. Ewings of this world capture the fancy of the public, justifying hatred for the rich. But this caricature of the rich is unjust, and equity calls for truth in the way we look at people. The biblical call to equity is a call to understanding, to being open and loving to members of all other political and economic camps. Such equity is essential to a just and prosperous nation.

The dream of an egalitarian society made possible by coercive policies of transfer or redistribution of wealth is not only unjust, but also ineffective. It has been argued that free enterprise gives out uneven slices of the doughnut while socialism hands out equal portions of the hole. This aphorism views the trend in redistributionist societies toward a net loss in national wealth. Transfer societies penalize achievement and subsidize inefficiency. Where free competition tends toward excellence and increased production, the policies of transfer encourage dependence on government subsidies and a dehumanizing addiction to welfare. The builder, the entrepreneur, the super-producer are stifled by government intervention.

The Redistribution of Wealth

In its inception the United States represented a political and economic experiment built on a system of free enterprise. Freedom was understood to involve free exchange in the market-place, freedom to produce, and freedom to enjoy the fruits of one's production. Economic freedom was viewed as essential to political freedom. But the watershed economic crisis of the Great Depression led to a redefinition of freedom. Its aftermath left people hungry for freedom from want and insecurity. Government intervention became the order of the day as Keynesian theory became a political and economic reality.

The Great Depression was nearly the downfall of our free enterprise system. Citizens began to doubt the market system. They were convinced it had failed, causing raging unemployment, home foreclosures, bank closings, and hunger. With only 150 years of history behind it, the nation was now hesitant to continue the grand experiment. The New Deal effort to restore the collapsing economy brought unprecedented levels of government regulation, taxation, and inflationary policies. Government mushroomed through the creation of new federal agencies. This was not viewed as a repudiation of free-market economics, but as a necessary adjustment to see the nation through a crisis in a boom/bust cycle.

However, the post-Depression adjustment turned out not to be temporary. New policies and the new definition of freedom created new expectations. The principle of limited government with limited involvement in the marketplace was gradually outrun in the political race to win more votes with promises of greater government benefits. Slowly, but inexorably, the transition to a transfer society set in. In 1960, federal, state, and local expenditures on social welfare programs totaled $52 billion. In 1965 the figure reached $77.2 billion. In 1975 these expenditures equaled $286 billion. Today transfer payments are over $500 billion.

There is still a margin of free enterprise in the United States, but that margin is rapidly shrinking to the diminishing point. We live in a nation of increasing wealth transfer. Socialism as an economic policy is no longer creeping; it is up and running. The federal government is by far the nation's largest employer. (Imagine for a moment the sheer magnitude of a government that has a $200-billion deficit!) The amount of power now held by the state is so immense that it is virtually unfathomable.

The folly of replacing equity with equality is perilous to the nation's economy. A system based on redistribution leads to economic and political horror. Soviet history makes this point vividly. The failures of the Soviet economy are not due to a failure in applying Marx's ideals. They are due to the country's success in applying them. Under socialism, the rich get poorer and the poor get poorer. Under capitalism, the rich get richer and the poor get richer. Equity gravitates toward prosperity; equality tends to poverty.

The paycheck we bring home is our profit. We trade our skills for our wages. Let us assume that our skills are in great demand, so our profit is substantial. Someone else, a person of low skill, brings home very little profit because his skills are not in great demand. The beneficent government, seeing the gross inequality of income between us, steps in with the graduated income tax. The second man is put on the rolls of four or five government programs. Money is redistributed. We are now on a relatively equal plane of wealth or poverty, depending on whether we see the cup as half full or half empty.

When profit is destroyed through redistribution, so also is the national wealth. Not only is the high-profit taxpayer hurt, but the recipients of equality-producing programs are hurt as well. Profit was the first of our five ingredients for material prosperity. When profit goes, so does material prosperity. Money taken by the government cannot be invested privately. Without that private investment, the poor man's skills will remain in low demand as industries shut down and unemployment rises. Government programs designed to make the people more equal only hurt the entire nation.

Profit is the goose that lays the golden eggs. It provides incentive to work, it allows for investment, and it is the basis for all trade. Killing the goose to divide it equally among our citizens may provide us with one glorious banquet today, but it ensures starvation tomorrow. As long as profit is taxed away in the name of equality, the goose can lay no more golden eggs. It is strangled. There is no incentive, and there is no capital for future investment.

The destruction of our national wealth will continue as long as there are those who can sell equality. To legislators and bureaucrats, the death of the golden goose is a blessing. Those in power who proclaim their hopes and plans for the end of poverty are the very persons who benefit from its continuation! An end to poverty would be the end of jobs for those who sell the economics of equality. Politicians step onto their soapboxes, promising more and more government money for poverty programs. The programs are born, profit is taxed, poverty grows, new programs are formed, more profits are taxed, and more people are poor. The process goes on and on, the welfare rolls swell, and the votes pour in for the humanitarian politicians who promise the most programs. These pimps of poverty make their living by creating more poor and then promising to help them with more poverty-inducing programs. The goose is gasping for breath. The more it falters, the more the poor will line up to vote for their newest savior.

As their promises grow to newer heights, politicians thrive on the failures of their own bad economic systems. In 1983, entitlement dollars spent for program administration—chiefly for the salaries of government employees—averaged $35,000 per person on welfare, a sum equal to three times the poverty level of income. The tragedy is that the purchasing power of the dollar owned by the poor man is diminished precisely by the programs designed to aid him.

Christians often bring up the Year of Jubilee as a defense for the policy of redistribution. But the Year of Jubilee was not a policy of redistribution of wealth. It was an early example of the renting of property. Leviticus 25:11–16 tells how the Year of Jubilee was to work.

> The fiftieth year shall be a jubilee for you; do not sow and do not reap what grows of itself or harvest the untended vines. For it is a jubilee and is to be holy for you; eat only what is taken directly from the fields. In this Year of Jubilee everyone is to return to his own property. If you sell land to one of your countrymen or buy any from him, do not take advantage of each other. You are to buy from your countryman on the basis of the number of years since the Jubilee. And he is to sell to you on the basis of the number of years left for harvesting crops. When the years are many, you are to increase the price, and when the years are few, you are to decrease the price, because what he is really selling you is the number of crops. (NIV)

If a man had ten daughters and one son, he had difficulty farming his land. If another man had ten sons, he was able to farm his own land and more. The man with many daughters rented his land to the man with many sons. The fifty-year period of Jubilee allowed for the passing of generations so that families could start over. The land was eventually restored to its original owner, but the renter was allowed to keep profits he made while farming it. No masses were counting down the years until they could reclaim what some unethical corporation had taken from them. No coercive transfer mechanism was involved. The idea behind Jubilee was to make the inheritance, the Promised Land, permanent and at the same time productive. Its intention was to protect private property, not abolish it. Jubilee allowed for the free market to work in the Promised Land. It was not a program of redistribution.

Nine

Government Force and Personal Freedom

Government equals force. This equation is so elementary it is easily obscured by the complexities of government theories. We tend to think of force in purely negative terms, associating it with a particular form of government such as tyranny. Yet it is vital for us to realize that all government, by its very nature, involves establishing a legalized system of force. Whether its form is monarchy, totalitarianism, or democracy, government is force.

It is easy to think that, in a free democratic society, government is not force. Democracy bases its existence on the consent of the governed; government leaders come into office through elections, not bloody coups; laws are passed through free legislative action moderated by various types of checks and balances; taxes are paid freely, without confiscation. What remains obscured by political rhetoric is that even in a free society, where democratic government is based on the consent of the governed, what the governed consent to must be government by force. Violations of laws enacted in such a society are met through force by arrest or detention. If the taxpayer refuses to pay his taxes, his taxes will be confiscated. This is force.

Recently a prominent United States senator made the casual remark at lunch in the Senate dining room, "I do not believe the government ever has the right to coerce anyone to do anything." That statement is astonishing. If taken literally, it can only mean that no government ever has the right to govern. But without coercion government has no means of law enforcement. As its root indicates, enforcement involves force. The power of such a government would be limited to offering suggestions. At best it would only be able to counsel or advise its citizens to behave in certain ways. In such a schema, taxes would be turned into free-will offerings.

Force, of course, is a general term, a genus with a wide variety of species. There are different kinds, different levels, and different degrees of force. Police brutality, for example, is a kind of excessive force, an abuse of the right of coercion. Force can obviously be misused to inflict injustice on people such as when parental force results in child abuse or the misuse of governmental force results in oppression. There may be a big difference in the ways a democracy and a dictatorship use force, but we must keep in mind that both are governments and therefore both use force.

The Biblical Injunction

The word "force" is so loaded with negative connotations that it may be difficult to remain comfortable with the idea that it is not intrinsically bad. The Christian must keep in mind that government is ordained and instituted by God and established even before the fall of man. Adam and Eve were made governors over creation. In turn they were created under government, under the rule of God. When they transgressed against their Creator, they were forced to leave Eden. After their expulsion from the garden, God appointed an angel with a flaming sword to stand guard at the entrance to Eden lest

Adam seek to force his way back to paradise. "So he drove out the man; and he placed at the east of the garden of Eden Cherubims, and a flaming sword which turned every way, to keep the way of the tree of life" (Gen. 3:24).

Theology must always include a vital concern about government. Giants of Christian theology have dealt with the role of civil government under the sovereign authority of God, concerning themselves with questions about what constitutes a just and legitimate government. Augustine, for example, argued that government is not so much a necessary evil as an institution made necessary by evil. It is because of sin that human government is necessary. Sin is a destructive force by which we violate other people and nature itself. The principal purpose of government is to restrain evil.

Augustine also grappled with the role of government in protecting human happiness. Stressing that happiness is ultimately rooted in a proper relationship with God, he recognized that at the same time human happiness can be thwarted by crimes committed against us. (When my family is victimized by theft or murder and when I am defrauded in my business enterprises, my pursuit of happiness is frustrated.) Augustine believed that the role of government is to restrain those evil forces robbing people of happiness in this world.

In the area of political theory, Martin Luther's work has occasioned much controversy. Luther has been credited with everything from foreshadowing Hegel and totalitarian fascism to being a prime architect of the principle of separation of church and state. Whatever the case, Luther maintained that the secular state was divinely ordered, and he stressed the duty of God-fearing citizens to fulfill their obligation of civil obedience.

With his support of civil government as a divine institution, John Calvin followed in the tradition of Augustine and Luther. Like the others, Calvin took his point of departure from the pivotal New Testament teaching on the state:

Let every soul be subject unto the higher powers. For there is no power but of God: the powers that be are ordained of God. Whosoever therefore resisteth the power, resisteth the ordinance of God: and they that resist shall receive to themselves damnation. For rulers are not a terror to good works, but to the evil. Wilt thou then not be afraid of the power? do that which is good, and thou shalt have praise of the same: for he is the minister of God to thee for good. But if thou do that which is evil, be afraid; for he beareth not the sword in vain: for he is the minister of God, a revenger to execute wrath upon him that doeth evil. Wherefore ye must needs be subject, not only for wrath, but also for conscience sake. For for this cause pay ye tribute also: for they are God's ministers, attending continually upon this very thing. Render therefore to all their dues; tribute to whom tribute is due; custom to whom custom; fear to whom fear; honour to whom honour.

Romans 13:1–7

The apostle Peter echoes Paul's teaching:

Submit yourselves to every ordinance of man for the Lord's sake: whether it be to the king, as supreme; or unto governors, as unto them that are sent by him for the punishment of evildoers, and for the praise of them that do well. For so is the will of God, that with well doing ye may put to silence the ignorance of foolish men: as free, and not using your liberty for a cloke of maliciousness, but as the servants of God. Honour all men. Love the brotherhood. Fear God. Honour the king.

1 Peter 2:13–17

In these verses we hear a strong admonition to the Christian to render respectful civil obedience. These passages make it virtually impossible for a Christian to embrace anarchy. Yet this stress on civil obedience does not mean the Christian may never disobey the government. There are times when the Christian citizen not only may, but must, disobey civil authorities.

The circumstances for justifiable civil disobedience will be explored later. First we must seek to understand the biblical stress of positive obedience.

Positive Obedience

Peter's statement that we are to submit ourselves to the authorities for "the Lord's sake" helps us understand why civil obedience is imperative. The kingdom of God is, in a very real sense, a political structure. It involves the seat of cosmic, governing authority. The title ascribed to Jesus, "King of Kings and Lord of Lords," not only is an exercise in laudatory expression but is rooted in concrete reality. All authority in heaven and in earth has been given by God the Father to God the Son. Christ is established at the right hand of God as the supreme governor of the universe. All lesser authorities are subject to him. If this were not so, then the biblical confession of the lordship of Christ would be devoid of meaning.

A sin against earthly authority is a sin against the cosmic crown adorning the head of Christ. Wanton disobedience of or disrespect toward earthly authorities reflects on the authority that stands over and above them. To have a cavalier attitude toward the local dogcatcher is to insult the majesty of Christ to whom the dogcatcher is ultimately accountable.

The New Testament injunctions about civil obedience are responses to the worldwide problem of lawlessness. Evil is not merely a local, isolated, or particular phenomenon because every act of wickedness ripples out from its center to spill into a wide area of life. The spirit of lawlessness lurks behind our every sin. Each sin is an act of lawlessness against God and adds to the total complex of evil. Since our fallen nature is given to lawlessness, every human being participates in this complex. Even the supreme, quintessential representative of all evil is called "the man of lawlessness" (2 Thess. 2:3 NIV).

It is not strange that the New Testament is somber in its warnings to be scrupulous in our obedience to authority.

Justifiable Disobedience

In spite of the strong admonitions to civil obedience, there are occasions in the New Testament when the Christian not only may but must disobey the civil authorities. The principle guiding us in this issue is both simple and clear: We are called to disobey the civil authorities whenever they command us to do something God forbids or forbid us to do something that God commands. If obedience to the civil authorities entails disobedience to God, we must obey God rather than men. If the civil authority commands us to steal or to murder, we must disobey. If the civil authority forbids the preaching of the gospel, we must nevertheless continue to preach the gospel.

What if civil laws inconvenience or oppress me? Here the applications become excruciatingly difficult. To disobey the speed limit merely because it inconveniences me is to add to the complex of lawlessness. But if the government oppresses us—if it, for example, imposes an oppressive tax burden—are we called to docile compliance? On this, students of Christian ethics disagree. On the one hand, the Bible clearly tells us to pay our taxes. The New Testament gives such instructions in the context of the Roman Empire, which placed a heavy tax burden on the Jews. To some Christians, there is little room for argument about the Christian's duty to pay his taxes. He may protest oppressive tax burdens by speaking out against them or by marching in a peaceful, nonviolent demonstration in front of the White House or the Internal Revenue Service. In the meantime, he must keep paying his taxes. Other Christians, however, argue to the contrary. They focus on the biblical instruction to pay taxes to those to whom taxes are due (see Matt. 22:21; Rom. 13:7). The issue is then whether unjust taxes are ever due anyone. It is not always easy to know how to apply the straightforward, biblical principle on civil disobedience.

The Christian faces a dilemma: Civil governments, though ordained by God, can become demonized, instruments of terror, injustice, oppression, and wickedness. Instead of promoting the general peace, they can promote violence. Instead of safeguarding the sanctity of life, they can destroy it either directly or by permissive legislation (as in the case of legalized abortion). Instead of protecting private property, these governments become the very instruments used to steal, confiscate, or redistribute it.

God gives civil governments the "power of the sword." With that power comes the responsibility to use the sword in the cause of justice. When civil magistrates use the sword as an instrument of injustice, not only are they doing violence to their victims, they are also rebelling against God and his Christ. The government's right to the sword is always circumscribed by justice. When the sword is used unjustly, the government has degenerated into tyranny.

These twin roles of government, protecting life and protecting property, are both intended to preserve freedom. The primary use of the sword is to protect, sustain, and maintain life. The government is called to restrain and punish those who would take the life of another by murder. The sword is to be used to defend the lives of the innocent and to punish the guilty, whether an aggressor nation or an individual murderer. The second responsibility of the government is to protect private property. The government may use forcible restraint to prevent robbery or vandalism. This responsibility goes beyond matters of direct and outright theft. Fraud in the marketplace violates private property rights, and the government should work to prevent such fraud. Government force then is to be used to restrain other forces that would violate personal life and property. When the government itself uses force to violate these, it becomes the criminal it has been ordained to restrain.

Freedom Redefined

Liberty is the central and crucial principle in the American dream of democracy. Freedom has been the most celebrated virtue in our national heritage. The Constitution promises our citizens the rights to life, liberty, and the pursuit of happiness. Our Pledge of Allegiance declares that we stand for liberty and justice for all. Our national anthem calls America the "land of the free." Freedom is our heritage, won by the blood of our fathers and guaranteed by our Constitution.

As we discussed in chapter 8, a subtle but powerful change in the meaning of freedom emerged in our culture in the thirties, as a result of the economic upheaval of the Great Depression. Under the New Deal, President Roosevelt introduced a new concept of freedom: *freedom from want*. This new ideal made it acceptable to compromise classical rights. The government stepped in to free people from poverty and financial insecurity, enacting new measures to secure economic security. Unfortunately, these guarantees necessitated programs aimed at redistributing wealth. The poor were now "entitled" to a certain level of financial security, even if it required the use of government force to impose unjust taxation on the wealthy. The government embraced a legalized Robin Hood policy.

This new definition of freedom had no historical precedent. In Europe, freedom has historically been equated with local national government, meaning that first of all a country would not be ruled by a foreign power. France was free under the emperor Napoleon since no foreign power controlled the government. The new American definition took the concept further. Now freedom meant that no government, including our own, should interfere unnecessarily in the lives of its citizens.

This freedom was guaranteed by the power of the vote. Private citizens could now help form policies with all the power of government force behind them. Paradoxically, the power to vote could destroy freedom as well as guarantee it, if voters enacted their own special interests without regard to justice and righteousness. The use of government force to enhance special interest, without regard to the rights of the minority, is an abomination to God.

Christians may not exercise their right to vote in order to steal from others. But surely they don't do this, do they? Yes, every day in a multitude of ways. The Christian who votes for measures that subsidize his business is using his ballot to take money from someone else and underwrite his own program. The parent who applies for a government loan to pay his child's education is using government force to take money from some private individual to pay for his child's education. Most Christians wouldn't think of going to their neighbors with a gun and demanding payment for their child's college education, but they will vote for such entitlements, forgetting that someone must be standing at their neighbors' door with a gun to insure the tax dollars will be there to provide for the loan.

With this redefinition of freedom, the government has undertaken a new series of responsibilities. Today our citizens expect the government to provide for their economic security. They assume it is the government's responsibility to insure the success of their businesses. Farmers march on Washington demanding price floors, parity programs, and other forms of subsidization. Unemployed laborers demand jobs or job-training programs. Business executives demand more tariffs and trade barriers. Scientists and artists clamor for money for their research and cultural enrichment programs. And while public television programs still solicit funds through charitable contributions, the trend today is toward finding support through government grants. This new freedom, the freedom from want, finds our government using its sword to cut cheese and butter and to turn over crops. The sword guards our borders not so much from the invasion of foreign armies as from the invasion of foreign autos, steel, and electronics.

As our wants grow, so grows our government. There is no ceiling to possible wants, so a government promising freedom from want has a big job. It is not strange that, since freedom has been redefined, the growth of government has been exponential. But as government grows, our freedom fades proportionately. With each new government program comes an automatic and irresistible loss of private freedom. The constitutional system of checks and balances designed to retard growth in government power is no longer able to do so effectively.

Most of our citizens do not seem to fear the loss of economic freedom. The carrot of economic security has become too appealing. Apparently they assume that as long as their political freedom is intact, economic freedom will remain intact, too. This fallacy is as deadly as it is seductive. Economic and political liberty may be distinguished but never separated. They are bound up with one another.

Consider, for example, the freedom of the press. Soviet Russia had no laws governing what the press could or could not write. While the Soviet constitution guaranteed freedom of the press, all legal Soviet printing presses were owned by the government. As a result, nothing bad was said about the Russian government. With no economic freedom of the press, there can be no political freedom of the press either.

At present there is no widespread protest in America about the loss of political and economic freedoms. If this erosion of liberty had happened suddenly and dramatically, there would undoubtedly have been riots in the streets and a call to arms. But the gradualism of the change has left us much like the proverbial frog who is warmed so slowly that he lethargically fails to jump out of the pan before the water boils. We have a national sense of security and well-being about living in a democracy rather than in communist China, Cuba, or North

Korea. We see the obvious differences between the methods of force employed in communist countries and those used in socialist countries. But lest we view these differences from a Pollyanna perspective, we must keep in mind that the ballot is a bullet. Laws established by vote carry no less force behind them than the decrees of a dictator. The dictator's guns fire the same kind of bullets as the guns used by law enforcement agencies in democratic nations. Both political structures make abundant use of prisons. Tyranny can exist in either form of government.

Warning Signals

More than thirty years before the American Revolution, Montesquieu's landmark work in France, *The Spirit of Laws,* set forth the thesis that there are basically three types of government: dictatorships, monarchies, and democracies. Through historical induction, he tried to discover the distinguishing characteristics of each of these forms. In dictatorships, Montesquieu reasoned fear as the indispensable element of continuity, that is, the dictator depends on the power of fear to keep his subjects paralyzed. Bloody purges and secret police action are a dictator's necessary tools to keep power. If the populace ever overcomes this fear enough to rise up against him, the dictator is threatened. (No dictator can afford a Lech Walesa running around loose in his domain.) On the other hand, monarchy does not rest on fear. Its chief necessary factor for continuity is honor. The social structure of lords and ladies, the pomp and circumstance of regal ceremony, the elaborate costumes (regalia) of the ruling bodies are all vital to maintaining a cultural milieu in which a monarchy can flourish. The word "courtesy" derives from the word "court" and describes the behavior appropriate around royalty. The touchstone of courtesy is honor. The ruffian who knows no courtesy, who eschews honor, is the figure representing the greatest threat to monarchy. In his analysis of democracy, Montesquieu singled out civic righteousness as the absolute prerequisite to survival of the system. He understood the power of the ballot and the potential problems created by tyranny of the majority. If the democracy is to survive, its laws must reflect righteousness rather than special interest. Montesquieu further argued that if one of the above systems collapses, it is usually replaced by one of the other two. Monarchy is not a great threat nowadays, but if democracy collapses for want of civic righteousness, what prevents its being replaced by a dictatorship?

Alexis de Tocqueville issued similar admonitions in the nineteenth century. He warned that two great threats hovered over the nascent, American republic. The first was that people would discover that the vote was worth money, that is, the potential for bribery, graft, and political corruption was built into any system involving courting votes as a necessary stepping stone to power. The second great threat was that people might vote themselves largesse. Once people discovered they could use the government to enrich themselves, the seed of democratic destruction would be sown.

The most crucial safeguard against both of these threats was the law. Since the time of ancient Greece, the most vital ingredient to a free society has been found in its lawcode. According to Frederic Bastiat, the final issue determining the survival of a free society is whether it is ruled by law or by men. This point is as critical as it is difficult to protect from confusion.

At first glance the terms "rule by law" and "rule by men" appear as a distinction without a difference. Is it not true that in a democratic society laws are made by men? The legislative bodies are composed of neither gods nor angels. Men enact the laws and men compose constitutions. Jefferson and Franklin were both mortals; Washington was from Virginia, not Mount Olympus. How then can Bastiat distinguish between rule by men and rule by law?

When the American republic was formed, there was a consensus that a nation's laws should be established upon some sort of higher law, a law transcending the interpretations and vested interests of individuals or groups. The higher law to which Jeffersonian democracy appealed was the *lex natura*, the law of nature. Philosophers, from Cicero and the Stoics down through the framers of British lawcodes, held that nature itself mirrors an ultimate law, the *lex supernaturalis*. Through the ages Christians, Jews, deists, and humanists have all sought an objective foundation for law, a foundation that would insure that Lady Justice's blindfold did not slip.

The breakdown of natural law as an objective safeguard to rule by men was hastened by the philosophical influence of American pragmatism. The thinking of William James, John Dewey, and Franklin Pierce built on Immanuel Kant's skepticism of man's ability to know anything of a transcendent nature. If God is unknowable to the human mind, then it follows that his transcendent law is equally unknowable. Once the foundation for the *lex aeternitatis* was attacked, the *lex naturalis* was left hanging in midair. Only a short time after Kant, the relevance of natural law to their area of concern was rejected by the majority of students of jurisprudence, so that today natural law is treated rarely, if ever, in American law schools.

When Oliver Wendell Holmes became the chief justice of the Supreme Court, he implemented a radically new philosophy of law. Holmes held that laws cannot reflect some nebulous transcendent norm of religious or philosophical truth, but must always reflect the desires of the contemporary community. Here is the clearest expression of rule by men that can be found in the annals of American jurisprudence. Holmes's work was a watershed marking the transition from rule by law to rule by men. This transition is substantive as it gives license to the tyranny of the majority.

The fruit of this legal pragmatism is called law positivism. Law positivism simply means that particular laws are all we ultimately have. There are no transcendent norms. There is no absolute law. Whatever the majority desires becomes law. In this schema it is possible to reinterpret the Constitution to bring its application into conformity with current community standards. Current community standards, of course, can support pornography, abortion, and a host of other highly controversial legal issues. In effect the Constitution's posture as the supreme sentinel for rule by law is broken. More importantly, justice is destroyed by the tyranny of the majority. We have reaped the fruit of Holmes's folly ever since.

Ten

Reinventing Government

In a class on communication skills I had in seminary we often played the synonym game. A student was given a rather ordinary word and had to come up with three better synonyms in ten seconds. "Rain" became "downpour," "torrent," "a visit from Jupiter Pluvious." I recall a particular phrase that expressed the folly of doing that which had been done before. Preaching to a congregation on the need to attend church was "bringing coals to Newcastle." That doesn't mean much unless one knows that Newcastle was the coal capital of England. A more common phrase to express the same idea is "reinventing the wheel." Such a notion has a negative connotation. It is repetitive, wasteful, redundant.

President Clinton and Vice President Gore, however, have pledged to "reinvent government." This endeavor has received nearly unanimous praise. Their goal is to streamline, to make the government more efficient. That government is wasteful and inefficient is universally recognized. It would seem to make sense to wade into the ocean of departments, bureaus, administrations, agencies, and filter out what is profligate and redundant. Why then are some conservatives not pleased with this leaning toward leanness?

Many are just skeptical. They point to Vice President Al Gore's record as a senator. As recently as 1990, Mr. Gore was rated by the National Taxpayers Union as the biggest spender in the Senate. They note also that the proposal was submitted after the budget had already passed. None of the ideas in the proposal are part of Clinton's "bare bones" budget. Finally, nothing in the proposal suggests how these ideas will become a reality. Congress must approve these changes, and has historically been reluctant to do so.

It has been said that President Clinton's strength is as a campaigner, not as a leader. Seeking to harness that strength, he and the vice president have traveled the country to raise support for the proposal. This also raises some skeptical eyebrows as we watch these two men flying hither and yon in government jets, retinue in tow, at a cost of $650,000 a day, "streamlining" government. The fear is that this is smoke and mirrors, an attempt to reposition the administration as "new Democrats," in favor of fiscal responsibility as they expand government to new, even more gargantuan, proportions.

To begin to "reinvent" government we first must know what government is. At the federal level government consists of three branches, the judiciary, the legislature, and the executive. When the founding fathers wrote our Constitution they sought to create a system whereby each branch was restrained from growing in size and scope by the other branches. Each was given specific tasks, and restrained from co-opting the tasks of the other branches. The restraining was even more severe vertically. The Constitution very clearly emphasizes that the federal government is only to be engaged in those tasks specifically assigned to it in the Constitution. If it's not mentioned, the federal government is to keep its hands off. Perhaps what we need is not to reinvent government, but to uninvent it.

Reinventing the Judiciary

The function assigned to the judicial branch was twofold. They were to interpret law, and mete out justice. Having been given the keys to the gate in interpreting the Constitution the Supreme Court would seem the least likely group to overextend their reach. That the justices are not elected and serve life terms would seem to be a hedge against the temptation to follow the whims of the moment. These nine people serve as the last defenders of the rights of the individual against the majority. In times past the court actually practiced this role. Franklin Roosevelt's New Deal sought to expand greatly the powers of the federal government. Several of his programs were declared unconstitutional. Roosevelt attempted to circumvent these roadblocks by packing the court, adding to the number of justices. This too was defeated.

Not content in its role as constitutional policeman, the court has of late engaged in activism. They have taken it on themselves to make law, not just interpret it. Perhaps the most infamous case is Roe v. Wade in which the court created an amorphous "right to privacy." Even the court recognized that such a right could not be pinpointed in the Constitution, claiming it was "assumed" either in the ninth or fourteenth amendments.

The courts have not only begun to legislate, they have actively engaged in enforcing the law, a role that is supposed to be the exclusive province of the executive branch. In countless cases the courts have ordered that prisons be built, and that budgets be allocated in particular ways. They have even gone so far as to order particular school districts to allocate funds to particular schools.

Reinventing Congress

"There oughtta be a law." When confronted with seeming injustice this is a common plea. The fact is, there probably is a law. There probably is a law forbidding whatever it is that may have irked us, but there is probably also a law commanding whatever it is that irked us. Probably the only thing the legislature does better than spend our money is pass mountains and mountains of laws, usually confusing, often contradictory.

Many Christians feel overwhelmed when, seeking to read and study the whole of God's Word, they find themselves confronted with page after page of case law in the Pentateuch. Nevertheless, the law contained in the Pentateuch was finite. God set up no legislative branch in establishing a government over his chosen nation. He gave them all the law they would need. The United States legislature, however, reconvenes every year and gives us more and more laws. Each year they seem to break records for the number of bills that have become law. The next several years should be no exception with both arms of the legislature controlled by the party of the president. No more gridlock in Washington means more gridlock in our lives.

The reason for the difference between Israel and America is clear. In Israel the law was established to promote justice. In America the law is established to promote the lawmakers. If I have the power to make people do what I wish them to do, I have the power to retain that power. If I am the senator from North Carolina I have the power to take money from people in Wyoming and give it to the tobacco farmers in my state. Those farmers appreciate my efforts, and so not only vote for me, but donate to my campaign so that I am better able to persuade others to vote for me. The people of Wyoming do not get a vote. Most of them do not even know that the money they work for is being handed over to tobacco farmers. They probably think their money is going to pay for governmental advertisements that try to persuade people not to use tobacco. Wyoming's senator may even support the transfer of payments to North Carolina, provided of course the senator from North Carolina will support the taking of money from the good people of North Carolina to pay for a new hydro-electric plant in Wyoming. This of course is not reinventing anything, it is a continuing exhibition of robbing

Peter to pay Paul and Paul to pay Peter, with a healthy cut for the broker and thanks from both Peter and Paul for the generosity of the robber.

Like the judicial branch the legislature is treading on the domains of other branches. Perhaps the most infamous example is "special prosecutor." This curious species is charged with investigating alleged misdoings of members of the executive branch. Investigation is properly the function of the executive branch. When Congress was not satisfied with the findings in the Iran-Contra scandal they set up their own investigation, granting Lawrence Walsh a virtually unlimited budget and unlimited time to make a case against former president Reagan and his aides. After millions of dollars and years of study Mr. Walsh came up with nothing.

This hybrid creation drew the ire of congressional conservatives who noted that the Constitution made no provision for a special prosecutor answerable only to Congress. When President Clinton found his feet in the fire for his business dealings while governor of Arkansas, however, many of the same conservatives called for a special prosecutor. The liberals, of course, would have none of it. What we end up with then is the right accusing the left of hypocrisy and the left accusing the right of hypocrisy. The result is the freak occurrence of both sides being right.

It doesn't take scandal for Congress to be butting into the affairs of the executive branch. Their assorted committees and subcommittees indulge in this at all times. Some subcommittees give orders to various cabinet agencies. The Veterans Administration, for instance, which has more than 200,000 employees, must receive congressional approval to fire just three workers. The Pentagon receives more than 100,000 congressional inquiries a year. In the late 1970s the Pentagon had to deal with four separate subcommittees who wrote defense legislation. Now they must deal with 24 committees and 40 subcommittees. It seems that even bureaucrats must deal with bureaucrats. Somehow it's not much consolation.

Who is responsible for all this oversight? How is it that 535 legislators can pass so many laws, and still find time to serve as executives? Staff. Congressional staffs have grown at an alarming rate. Between 1970 and 1992 the total number of federal employees rose from 2.1 million to 2.2 million, an increase of 4.8 percent. At the same time, however, Congress nearly doubled in size. The House of Representatives employed 7,022 people in 1970. By 1980 that number had grown to 11,406. In 1992 the total was 12,236. Of those 12,236 employees, exactly 535 were elected to pass laws. The rest are just expenses.

The Senate has not done as well in keeping down payroll and expenses. In 1970 the Senate employed 4,105 people. Since we suffered from a dearth of laws back then the Senate went on a hiring spree. In 1980 they employed 6,995 people. Twelve years later the figure had reached 7,820 employees. The increase over those 22 years was 90.5 percent.

All these people, of course, cost money. In 1970 Congress spent $343 million in running its operations. In 1980 the cost had risen to $1.2 billion. Twelve years later the cost had risen to $2.8 billion. This paid not only for the 20,000 House and Senate staffers, but also for the 18,000 staffers in the Congressional Budget Office, the General Accounting Office, the Library of Congress, and other congressional agencies.

In 1960 the average member of Congress managed to do his or her job with only 9 staffers. In 1992 the average had risen to 28. What are all these people doing? The argument is made that all these staffers are necessary to oversee the vast executive branch activities. The reality is that the bulk of these new employees spend their time in the home state of the Congress member. They are assigned to "constituent service." Their job is to see that everyone is happy, from the little old lady whose social security check is late to the local businessman who needs a federal job or two to prosper. In 1972 an eighth of Senate staffers and a fourth of their House counterparts worked from their home states. In 1990 those numbers had changed. A third of Senate staffers and 40 percent of House staffers now work in their home states. Personal service for future voters, provided at the taxpayers' expense, is only one way to further entrench an already entrenched Congress.

How well are these staffs doing their jobs? In light of the "health care crisis" and impending health care legislation, syndicated columnist Matthew Lesko recently polled 100 congressional offices. He found that 71 of them, nearly three fourths, were unaware of existing federal programs that provide health care for the uninsured. The Hill-Burton program, for instance, requires hospitals and nursing homes to provide free care to those having trouble paying their bills. It seems that Congress is already busy "reinventing government"; they seem to have forgotten that they've already invented it.

Reinventing the Executive Branch

The executive branch is perhaps the most fearful arm of government. It is they who actually do things. It is their job to enforce the law, to carry it out. While they do not intrude into the judicial end of things, beyond their proper function of appointing justices, they have, of late, stepped over an important line of separation regarding the legislature. Recognizing that the chief executive, the president, is the single most powerful man in government, the founding fathers set some strict limits. The president is given virtually free rein in matters of foreign policy. The exception is in the declaring of war. Such an act requires an act of Congress, at least according to the Constitution. Not since World War II has this actually happened. In Korea, Vietnam, Grenada, Libya, Panama, Iraq, and

Somalia, U.S. soldiers took up arms, attacked other armies, and died in combat, all without a single declaration of war. Presidents Truman, Kennedy, Johnson, Nixon, Reagan, Bush, and Clinton have all "reinvented government," making war. They have snatched the prerogative of the legislature, and sent tens of thousands to their deaths.

It is the continuing war on freedom, however, in which the executive branch has expanded their powers. Not content to see to their constitutionally enumerated powers the executive branch has wheedled its way into nearly every part of our lives. They have not only stretched the grey areas, finding meager footholds to justify their intrusion, they have often directly violated the Constitution to enter into areas specifically forbidden to them.

Article 1, Section 8, clause 3 of the Constitution empowers the federal government to "regulate Commerce . . . among several states." It seems fairly clear. Imagine a farmer of dairy and poultry in Ohio. Each year he raised a small quantity of wheat, just enough for his family, his animals, and for seeding the next year's crop. Washington, in 1938, passed a law limiting the amount of wheat that could be planted. In 1941 our farmer exceeded that limit and was slapped with a penalty. He argued that the federal government had no jurisdiction over his wheat, since it was in no way connected to interstate commerce. The Supreme Court, in 1942, disagreed. It made a connection to interstate commerce by reasoning that if our farmer friend had not grown his own wheat, he might have bought wheat from another state. Not engaging in interstate commerce, the government concluded, means engaging in interstate commerce because if you didn't engage in interstate commerce, you would engage in interstate commerce. Is that perfectly clear?

Surely the government must have learned from such folly. Unfortunately, they have reinvented such stupidity time and again. Imagine another farmer, this one a farmer of peaches and nectarines in California. It is his intention to sell his crop to poor people in Los Angeles, many of whom are in dire straits because of the riots. Keep in mind that the producer produces in California, and the consumers will consume in California. Nevertheless, the federal government intervenes. Federal regulators, agents of the Department of Agriculture, order that millions of pounds of perfectly good fruit be dumped on the road and left to rot. Why? The peaches and nectarines are too small. Too small for what? The regulators don't say. They must be proud, though, saving the poor people of Los Angeles from the dreaded small fruit.

Surely these government follies are not deadly or even dangerous. I don't lie awake at night fearful that the government will take away my fruit. These examples, however, illustrate how far our government has run amuck. If we knew our Constitution, we would ask more basic questions. Why is the executive branch regulating agriculture at all? It is nowhere mentioned as a responsibility of the federal government. Why is there a department of education? Education is nowhere mentioned in the Constitution. How is it that the executive branch could even contemplate co-opting the entire health care business of the nation? Check the enumerated powers; regulating health care at all, let alone subsuming it, at least an eighth of the entire U.S. economy, is not a task assigned to the federal government.

Run down a list of cabinet level departments, and check which might even conceivably be connected to a constitutionally delegated power. Labor? Interior? Health and Human Services? Agriculture? Housing and Urban Development? Energy? Where in the Constitution is the federal government granted the right to take money from young people to give to retired people? Where in the Constitution is the government given the power to regulate banks? To insure banks? Where in the Constitution is the federal government given the right to regulate television and radio? Where is the executive branch charged with the task of building massive dams, or providing electricity to farmers? The executive branch knows no limits. It has stretched the Constitution to the point that there is literally nothing the government can't stick its hands into, for any reason.

How much is all this costing us? Trying to get a handle on the cost of government is almost as difficult as getting a handle on the scope of government. One way to measure the cost is by calculating the total tax burden. Early in this century all forms of government—local, state, and federal—consumed 6 to 7 percent of the gross national product (GNP is essentially the total value of all wealth produced in the nation in a given year). By 1950 that percentage had risen to 24. By 1990, total taxation reached 32 percent of GNP. Despite the self-congratulations of the Reagan administration total taxes actually rose slightly in the 1980s.

Perhaps a better standard of measurement is the total amount of government spending. Again in the early part of the century total spending amounted to about 6 or 7 percent of GNP. In 1950 all governments—local, state, and federal—spent about 21 percent of GNP. Forty years later total spending reached 34 percent of GNP. (The difference between taxation in 1990 of 32 percent and spending of 34 percent is deficit spending.) Understand that this means that of all the labor and effort that went into producing goods and services, of all the fruit of all the labor of every man, woman, and child, governments take one third. Understand also that these figures are from 1990, prior to the largest tax increase in history. Neither does it take into account the "non-taxes" the president plans to extort from employers for his heath care program.

This is by no means the total cost of government. Every regulation, whether it be the handiwork of the Congress or a minor bureaucrat in some department of the executive branch, adds costs to our lives. It is probably impossible to calculate the costs of the ocean of regulations burdening the economy. No one bothers to calculate losses such as fruit rotting on the streets because it is too small. Estimates begin in the hundreds of billions. Every analyst agrees that the number is only growing.

The executive branch is by and large responsible for this mess. Keep in mind that only the president is able to write the national budget. The gentleman who suggests that he would like to reinvent government may do so. He can also uninvent it. He has the power to dismantle the machine. He could fell the leviathan, were he so inclined. A good model to follow might be a little known document called the Constitution.

Reinventing Our Thinking

The final report of the National Performance Review led by Vice President Gore calls for "reinventing government." The report begins, "We spend $25 billion a year on welfare, $27 billion on food stamps, and more than $13 billion on public housing—yet more Americans fall into poverty every year. We spend $12 billion waging war on drugs—yet see few signs of victory. We fund 150 different employment and training programs—yet the average American has no idea where to get job training, and the skills of our workforce fall further behind those of our competitors." Despite this impressive track record of failure, the function of the report was not to study whether or not such programs are doomed to failure, but to try to learn to fail more efficiently. Certainly the American people would be far happier if the government failed with fewer dollars.

The report is very specific in its refusal to examine the appropriateness of these programs. It states, "Our job was to improve performance in areas where policymakers had already decided government should play a role." It goes on to decry that for "too long the basic functioning of the government has gone unexamined."

The problem, however, is not inefficiency. If my family found itself in debt because of fancy cars, vacations, jewels, and furs, the solution would not be using coupons when we shop for groceries. We are not in the mess we're in because Department of Agriculture bureaucrats destroy too small fruit inefficiently. The problem is our understanding of the function of government. As long as the government is seen as the solution to all of our problems the government will continue to be the source of many of our problems.

We do not need to reinvent government, but to rethink government. We need to tame the monster, and coax it back into its constitutional cage. We need to rethink how we see government. We need to see every intrusion into areas outside its role not as opportunities for personal profit, but as fearful movements toward statism. Until government performs its role of protecting our lives and property from harm, we can expect turmoil, interference, conflict, graft, and waste. It's not so much that government is lazy and wasteful as it is that government is nosy and presumptuous. Robert Welch was right when he said, "America would be better off with a government of three hundred thousand officials and agents, every single one of them a thief, than a government of three million agents with every single one of them an honest, honorable, public servant," since "the first group would only steal from the American economic and political system; the second group would be bound in time to destroy it."

Eleven

Where Are We Headed?

The Growth

The American economy is suffering from a growing rate of taxation brought about largely by the explosive growth of government and government spending. The growth of government can be seen in the fact that the current annual deficit is larger than the entire annual budget during Johnson's Great Society. From the start of the Carter administration to the first year of the Reagan administration, the annual deficit quadrupled. And the deficit has been increasing yearly. By 1983 the federal budget had climbed to $800 billion—an astronomical amount. By 1993 the budget was nearly twice as large, at $1.5 trillion and the federal debt (accumulated deficit) had reached $4 trillion! (To help you get a handle on the meaning of this, suppose that the day that Christ was born you had $1.5 trillion to spend without the benefit of daily compounded interest. You set about spending the principal at a rate of $2 million a day. If you spent $2 million a day, each day, by the year 2000 you would still have more than $50 billion left to spend.)

Every fiscal year, the president makes a projected budget. This must be approved by Congress. Each year the amount the government spends increases, as does the amount the government takes. Spending, however, is climbing at a faster rate than income. This is the cause of the deficit. Although it is customary for the president to promise a balanced budget, this has not been achieved in over thirty years, and prospects for the immediate future are grim. President Clinton's own numbers show that even if he passes his "deficit reduction package," and even if it does not slow the economy (as tax increases always do), we can still expect annual deficits over $225 billion. Deficits will probably go higher in the future as budgets bear the burden of keeping freedom from want alive, and as the government faces the interest on a four-trillion-dollar debt. The load of a mounting interest payment makes escape from the deficit extremely problematic.

Every dollar the government spends, whether it be for a welfare mother, a jobs program, or a B-2 bomber, must first be taken from the private sector. And the government has two primary sources for doing this: taxation and printing fiat money. (Issuing bonds is not a real source of income. Bonds are merely loans the government takes out on the American people, with the interest and the principal later paid by the citizens. They amount to the government's promise to tax or print in the future.) Projected income is the amount of money the government expects to take in during any given year. Taxation, equal to approximately 30 percent of the gross national product, is not enough to cover a year's projected and real spending. The difference is the deficit.

The government issues an order to the Federal Reserve for funds to cover the deficit. The funds are delivered via the printing press. This inflationary action is the government's second source of income, and it causes as much of a problem as the ballooning taxation. Since inflation devalues the currency, its net effect on the taxpayer is to reduce his purchasing power as much as or more than if the government had simply increased taxes to a higher rate.

But the government can only tax so much; wage earners know why their take-home pay is so much less than their gross income. Yet those who complain about their taxes can usually be counted on to clamor for more government programs to put more money into their pockets. Politicians cannot afford to alienate the legions of voters who want less taxation and more programs. The political solution to this dilemma? Deficit spending backed by an increased money supply. The loss of purchasing power due to a 30 percent increase in the money supply is much more difficult to see than the loss due to withheld taxes. But it is nonetheless real and painful, and it creates a vicious circle.

The Cost

Deficit spending works as long as the voting public remains ignorant of the true nature of inflation. As long as inflation is seen as a business problem or an entity with a life all its own, the government will be tempted to continue inflationary policies. It has our blessing to discourage saving, hinder capital investment, and otherwise take the vitality out of our national economy. The blame for inflation rests both on the shoulders of our government leaders and on the public who demand political promises from their candidates.

Special-interest groups play a significant role in deficit spending. A special-interest group is a block of voters who feel strongly about one issue and want government money for it. In exchange for votes and monetary support, a candidate for public office agrees to promote the special interest. These groups range in size from small, medical research groups to the National Education Association with its 1.7 million members. (The NEA threw its support and money behind presidential hopeful Jimmy Carter during the 1976 presidential campaign, and once in office Carter created a new cabinet-level department, the Department of Education.) Special-interest activity, in fulfillment of Alexis de Tocqueville's prophecy that democracy will work until people realize they can vote themselves largesse, pushes up government spending to newer heights, making deficit spending a political necessity. The price tag is staggering.

The government also runs up a large bill in support of private businesses. Low-interest loans to private businesses run the budget still higher. Business welfare is growing while the welfare of business is declining due to high taxes and an inflated money supply. From funding the continental railroad to sending up satellites to Ross Perot's billion-dollar data systems, the government is deep into the business of business. This unholy alliance distorts the market system and costs the taxpayer dearly.

Government intervention in the farming industry also costs the taxpayer. Rather than allowing farm products to be sold through free interaction between supply and demand, the government sets price floors. These artificially high prices dry up demand for the products. At other times price floors are replaced by outright subsidies to farmers. From 1986 to 1988 the federal government handed out $70 billion to farmers. The government also buys surplus agriculture. In December of 1986 the government had in storage 2.7 billion bushels of wheat, 10.3 billion bushels of corn, and 325 million bushels of oats and barley.

The government is also in the business of funding incompetence. In the interest of antimonopoly sentiments and misled patriotic feelings, the government now spends billions trying to revive already dead or moribund industries. The Chrysler Corporation, the third largest manufacturer of cars in the United States, is a good example. A few years ago it stood on the brink of bankruptcy. Because the public did not prefer its products in a competitive market, Chrysler was losing a great deal of money year after year. Most businesses that cannot sell their product, like Eastern Airlines, go out of business. This was not the fate of Chrysler, which received a generous, low-interest loan of $1.5 billion from our government. You and I and Henry Ford III—America's taxpayers—were forced to finance this bail-out. The money Chrysler received could have been used by productive businesses that were meeting the needs of the public. Had the money been left in the marketplace, it could have provided jobs for strong businesses. The loan did not save jobs; it merely transferred them. Government can only give that which it first takes.

The government has other means besides low-interest loans and grants to protect and aid incompetent industries. The tariff has long been used in America, not as a means of raising revenue, but to protect weak, domestic industries. Protective tariffs are a problem to every consumer in America. The fallacy of the protective tariff is an old one, one that Adam Smith refuted over two hundred years ago in *The Wealth of Nations:*

> In every country it always is and must be the interest of the great body of the people to buy whatever they want of those who sell it cheapest. The proposition is so very manifest that it seems ridiculous to take any pains to prove it; nor could it ever have been called in question, had not the interested sophistry of merchants and manufacturers confounded the common sense of mankind.[1]

Consider this illustration. Harley-Davidson is the last remaining producer of motorcycles in America but it has not built a better or cheaper motorcycle than its foreign competitors. Its only model costs $1,500, and a Japanese manufacturer can sell a motorcycle of the same quality for $1,250. Without a tariff, Harley-Davidson would soon be out of business, leaving workers unemployed. The government charges the Japanese producers $250 to sell their product in America. On the surface it appears that many American jobs are saved by the tariff. Are they?

Assume our government removes the tariff. Harley-Davidson goes out of business. Those who buy motorcycles now have 250 more dollars to spend elsewhere. This may mean one more job in one factory, or two in another. This money will create jobs, productive jobs, in competent businesses. In addition, the Japanese manufacturer will eventually spend his American dollars in America on businesses that are competent and that can produce something cheap and in demand, unlike Harley-Davidson. Ultimately tariffs do not save jobs, and they cost the consumer by benefitting only the noncompetitive business. The government cannot save one industry without in turn hurting hundreds of others.

The government is likewise guilty of costing the public billions of dollars annually through its practice of price-fixing. Price-fixing disrupts the basic components of the free market: supply and demand. Upon entering the marketplace, each consumer and producer arrives with his own value system. A roadside corn seller may wish to charge $22.50 a bushel for his corn but to no avail, consumers are unwilling to spend that much on corn. As with the bubble gum and baseball cards, transactions work best when left unhampered. The government can force the bubble gum seller to set a price, but it cannot force him to value his bubble gum less than he does or force a consumer to value it more. Such attempts will always backfire. Economic value is subjective and therefore not subject to government decrees.

The Road Ahead

The dismal science of economics rarely gives its students the opportunity to rejoice over new discoveries. The physicist who comes to a better understanding of electricity is able to contribute to a better light bulb. The chemist is able to produce a vaccine to aid in world health. The biologist may help develop a new high-protein grain. Economists enjoy no such discoveries.

Alvin Toffler's best-selling book, *The Third Wave,* predicts a bright future for the world based on technological advancements. Applied science will bring the world more and better food, more jobs, and increasing prosperity. Others predict cancer cures, higher crop yields, and more efficient light bulbs. However, economists of all sorts—liberals, conservatives, and moderates—predict only economic problems. Liberals clamor that any conservative tilt to an administration's economic policy will lead directly to economic disaster. At the same time conservatives attack the liberal aspects of the same administration's policy. Everyone hopes to gain prestige from predicting economic downfall, knowing full well that if the economy grows stronger no one loses. Perhaps it is not the science of economics that is so dismal—it is the economists themselves.

This book has examined those biblical principles that guide a proper study of economics. We have observed the dynamics of economic interaction, the tools necessary for economic prosperity, the relationship of supply and demand, the evolution of trade and money, the nature of profit, and the nature of government. We have seen the many ways the American government and governments abroad have wrongfully interfered with economic processes. We have examined some of the follies the government commits every day. And we have looked at destructive attitudes people have toward trade, profit, and saving.

When confronted with our present state of economic affairs, we must plan to avert these problems in the future. Many want to know what can be done to stop the rising tide of government spending, redistribution programs, inflation, and regulation. We Christians are in a delicate position. It is our duty to obey the government. We may not cheat on tax forms to protect what is rightfully ours. We may not disobey government regulations, no matter how destructive they may be. So what can we do?

The first step in stopping government growth is not to use government services. We pay taxes, so we want a return. We send our children to public schools, allow the government to finance our loans on college education, houses, and business improvements, and we buy government bonds. If the government is to be held in check, this must stop. Anyone dedicated to small government must stop using the government for his own personal gain.

Some hope to gain revenge by collecting as many government dollars as possible. The cost of such revenge is ultimately absorbed by other taxpayers and not by the government. Any money the government takes from you is gone, spent. Anything you receive, beyond protection of life and property, is taken from another unjustly. To stop incessant taxing and spending we must adopt a cheek-turning policy, and not one of an eye for an eye. We must remember that the government has no "eye" to take. We cannot punish the government by feeding at the public trough. We will only punish taxpayers.

Let's examine the social security program. Those dollars the government takes for your future are not really for your future; they are for someone else's present. Your monthly social security payment is spent by the time you pay the next month's payment. The government is not putting your money away in a bank account until you retire. The money goes to Washington to pay the salaries of the army of bureaucrats who run the system. What is left is quickly passed on to retirees across the nation. The money is gone. If you retire and receive social security, those who pay for it are still working. Social security is not a program of mandatory saving for old age; it is a program for the young, subsidizing the old.

If no one accepted government money, the federal budget would shrink to a reasonable size. We must avoid the attitude that if we don't take it, someone else will. We can effectively boycott government spending programs thus lowering taxation and inflation as well as improving the economy. Accepting wealth-transfer payments is a sin against taxpayers and God, a sin we can no longer afford to commit.

Today in America, our legal system is dominated by bureaucracy. Congress sets new records each year on the amount of legislation it passes, averaging about five hundred new laws a year. The real lawmakers, however, are the bureaucrats who have no system of checks and balances. Bureaucratic regulations, affecting millions, move from the bureaucrats' mouths to the law books. No one votes for these bureaucrats, and no one votes on the confusing and often contradictory rules they pump out. American citizens are not only saddled with the tyranny of majority via Congress, but also with the tyranny of bureaucracy. No one knows exactly how many laws are on the federal books.

In order for our country to enjoy the freedom and prosperity it once enjoyed, we need a major change in our law base. The law, which we as Christians are obligated to follow, is a hindrance to freedom. A proper, biblical law base is one that protects freedom, not one that destroys it. Our laws allow for paper money, confiscatory taxation, and overwhelming regulation. These laws must change before we can expect a brighter economic picture. The essence of government is law. When government goes bad, its laws go bad. As long as we sit passively while the government frantically pumps out more and more complex laws intruding on free movement in the marketplace, the only changes we can expect to see will be for the worse. While people march on Washington demanding more government redistribution, interference, and intervention, we sit in our easy chairs watching the evening news. We need active inaction on spending programs and active action on changing our law base.

The pleas are generally the same: "Write your legislators," "Support a candidate," "Run for office," "Join a committee." These calls come from all sides of the political spectrum and produce few results. We are involved in a war of ideas. The best weapon is not letter-writing or campaigning, but education. Public opinion is a strong force in America today. It is not swayed by political speeches; it is not swayed by burning editorials. Public opinion changes one mind at a time, through private conversations, one to one. Forget Emily Post and discuss politics. Each new convert to the cause of Christian freedom is another soldier in the war of ideas. To be effective, one must be educated—not necessarily with a degree in economics or political science, but with a clear understanding of the way the market works, the effects of government interference, and the biblical principles that relate to economics. An educated layman is more effective than ten economics scholars. But the most clear-thinking layperson is totally ineffective if he or she continues to use the government for private gain. Hypocrisy does not help the cause of freedom—education and dedication do.

Voting often presents an ethical dilemma. The first Tuesday following the first Monday of every November is a difficult time for many Christians. Rarely does a candidate have a platform that is entirely faithful to Scripture. Voting leaves us with three choices: We can vote for one of the two candidates offered; we can use the write-in process, saying no to both official candidates; or we can not vote at all. Voting for one candidate amounts to choosing the lesser of two evils. If one vote is an endorsement of the unbiblical, graduated income tax, and another vote is an endorsement of tariffs, for whom do you vote? Not voting endorses neither, but one still takes office. Not voting is one way to demonstrate displeasure with the available candidates. But not voting can easily be attributed to voter apathy rather than to voter anger. We are left with a difficult dilemma.

Recently there has been a great deal of talk but very little action concerning budget deficits. The adoption of an amendment to the Constitution requiring annually balanced budgets would have a significant effect on the economy. A balanced budget automatically eliminates inflation. The printing of fiat money would instantly cease, freeing more money for saving and therefore for increased capital investment. A balanced budget would dramatically hamper government spending. The government can only tax its citizens so much. Taxation beyond a certain point brings an angry reaction from voters. Politicians have gotten around this problem by paying for their pet programs with inflated dollars. That option is eliminated with a balanced budget amendment. With a political ceiling on tax rates and no inflation, government spending would have to go down, leaving money for production purposes in the marketplace. Passage of such an amendment would alert politicians that the American citizenry is tired of fiscal irresponsibility. It would alert our politicians that we are watching them and that they must respect our intelligence.

We need to support such an amendment vocally. A grass-roots support system would insure its passage in the near future. The sooner we have such an amendment, the sooner we can begin to build a strong, healthy economy. The importance of a balanced budget cannot be obscured. We must require our government to practice good stewardship, to practice sound house-rule. We must hold our government and ourselves accountable for spending more than we have. The power to inflate is a danger we cannot safely overlook.

We must actively work to stop government spending. The battle does not start in the media nor in the voting booths, but at home. Each government check that comes into our homes is a part of the problem. As long as there is a demand for government spending, the government will meet it, at the ultimate expense of the taxpayer. At home we can face the problem, not only by refusing government assistance but also by talking with friends and neighbors. We must educate ourselves and those around us. A small-government mind-set in America will produce small government. Ignorance, on the other hand, will allow the government to grow to bigger and more frightening proportions.

The pulpit is an excellent place for education. If our ministers fear to speak out against government growth, they soon may not enjoy the freedom at all. Holistic preaching demands that we approach the subject of public policy. God found it important enough to include it in the Scriptures, and we should be able to hear it in our churches.

What can we do? We can learn. We can teach. We can pray for our leaders. And we can face the issues and study them in light of God's Word. Prayer and education are the two strongest tools the Christian has. It is up to us to use them and to call our nation to true, national discipleship, under God, with liberty and justice for all.

Notes

Chapter 1—Hard Times—A Christian Approach

1. John Calvin, *Institutes of the Christian Religion, Vol. 1* (Philadelphia: Presbyterian Board of Christian Education, 1932), 371.

Chapter 3—Prosperity

1. Adam Smith, *An Inquiry into the Nature and Causes of Wealth of Nations* (New York: The Modern Library, 1900), 14.

2. Leonard Reed, *The Freedom Philosophy* (Irvington-on-Hudson, N.Y.: Foundation for Economic Education, 1988), 137–42.

3. William Simon, *A Time for Truth* (New York: McGraw-Hill Book Company, 1978), 92.

Chapter 4—Profit Is Not a Four-Letter Word

1. James Hastings, *Dictionary of the Bible, Vol. 1* (New York: Charles Scribner's Sons, 1898), 629.

Chapter 5—What Money Can Do

1. Paul Einzig, *Primitive Money* (London: Eyre and Spottiswoode, 1948), 198.

Chapter 6—The Inflationary Rip-Off

1. Garet Garrett, *The People's Pottage* (Caldwell, Idaho: Caxton Printers Ltd., 1965), 27.

2. *The American Heritage Dictionary of the English Language,* William Morris, ed. (Boston: Houghton Mifflin, 1981), 487.

Chapter 7—Biblical Concern for the Poor

1. Yehezkel Kaufmann, *The Religion of Israel* (Chicago: University of Chicago Press, 1960), 319–20.
2. Karl Barth, *Doctrine of Rehabilitation* (Edinburgh: T. & T. Clarke, 1956), 18.
3. Auberon Herbert, *The Right and Wrong of Compulsion by the State* (Indianapolis: Liberty Chimes, 1978), 77.
4. Murray Rothbard, *Man, Economy, and State* (Los Angeles: Nash Publishing Corporation, 1970), 818.
5. Ibid., 931.

Chapter 8—Equality vs. Equity

1. Philip Hughes, *Paul's Second Epistle to the Corinthians* (Grand Rapids: Wm. B. Eerdmans Publishing Company, 1962), 306.
2. J. B. Lightfoot, *Saint Paul's Epistles to the Colossians and to Philemon* (Grand Rapids: Zondervan, 1959), 210.
3. Ronald Nash, *Social Justice and the Christian Church* (Milford, Mich.: Mott Media, 1983), 31.
4. Ibid., 28–29.

Chapter 11—Where Are We Headed?

1. Adam Smith, *Wealth of Nations,* 424.

Index